More Praise for *Living in More Than One World*

"An indispensable addition to any Drucker library. Bruce Rosenstein takes a refreshing and innovative approach to reviewing Drucker's teachings and providing waypoints guiding readers through their own personal multidimensional journey through life. "

—Robert E. Gaylord, Brigadier General, U.S. Army (Retired), and President and CEO, IDEA

"Everyone is the CEO of his or her own life. Rosenstein's passionate application of Drucker's business ideas to managing our own lives is powerful and compelling."

—Rod Beckstrom, coauthor of *The Starfish and the Spider: The Unstoppable Power of Leaderless Organizations*

"*Living in More Than One World* succinctly captures Peter Drucker's timeless wisdom for a world that needs it more than ever. It is essential reading for leaders of today and tomorrow."

—Richard F. Schubert, former President, American Red Cross

"In this timely and important book, Bruce Rosenstein has synthesized some of my grandfather's most important messages for applying knowledge to the complex challenges we face today and, especially, in the future."

—Nova Spivack, CEO, Twine

"I was lucky to have known Drucker, and the experience changed my life in ways I can't begin to recount. Reading this book will do the same for you by offering a glimpse into the man who changed the way we think and talk about business!"

—Thomas Koulopoulos, founder, Delphi Group, and author of *The Innovation Zone*

"Drucker approached his life and his life's work in a manner quite unlike anything I'd witnessed before I was his student in the 1980s and his coworker in the 1990s. This book is an important piece of work, starting with our commitment to higher principles, extending into effective guardianship of scarce resources, and ultimately manifesting in the form of empowering service to others."

—Synthia Laura Molina, Managing Partner, Central IQ, Inc.

"In our world of economic turmoil, Bruce Rosenstein skillfully moves us toward a multidimensional life as exemplified by the great management philosopher, Peter Drucker, who lived what he preached. This journey will offer both personal transformation and a window through which to view one's legacy."

—Kathleen Horsch, Chairman, The Human Spirit Initiative

"Designing and shaping one's career and work-life balance is becoming increasingly difficult to achieve—Bruce Rosenstein has gone back to the 'Master' to look for answers. This book provides innumerable guidelines for all knowledge workers to organize their lives in an age of market, financial, and personal uncertainty."

—Jay Rao, Professor of Technology and Operations Management, Babson College

"Peter Drucker is the greatest management thought leader of all time. I had the good fortune to study with Drucker in graduate school. Rosenstein's book shows how classic Drucker principles can improve any knowledge worker's daily life."

—Geoff Smart, CEO, ghSMART, and *New York Times* bestselling coauthor of *Who: The A Method for Hiring*

"I've been fascinated with the human side of Peter Drucker's work for over thirty years. In my communications with him, he validated that leadership development, especially of knowledge workers, begins with personal development. Bruce captures Peter's core belief that being authentic is the highest form of emotional intelligence."

—Dr. Paul Wieand, Chairman and founder, The Center for Advanced Emotional Intelligence

"As 'the self-help book that Drucker never wrote,' *Living in More Than One World* fills an important gap in the personal development literature, impressively showing how we do not change the world, or even our own organization, until we have first worked on ourselves. A must-read for all who demand more of their personal and professional lives."

—Tom Butler-Bowdon, author of *50 Self-Help Classics, 50 Success Classics, 50 Psychology Classics*, and *50 Prosperity Classics*

Living in More Than One World

Living in More Than One World

How Peter Drucker's Wisdom
Can Inspire and Transform Your Life

Bruce Rosenstein

BK

Berrett–Koehler Publishers, Inc.
San Francisco
a BK Life book

Berrett-Koehler Publishers, Inc.
235 Montgomery Street, Suite 650
San Francisco, CA 94104-2916
Tel: (415) 288-0260   Fax: (415) 362-2512   www.bkconnection.com

Ordering Information

Quantity sales. Special discounts are available on quantity purchases by corporations, associations, and others. For details, contact the "Special Sales Department" at the Berrett-Koehler address above.

Individual sales. Berrett-Koehler publications are available through most bookstores. They can also be ordered directly from Berrett-Koehler:
Tel: (800) 929-2929; Fax: (802) 864-7626; www.bkconnection.com

Orders for college textbook/course adoption use. Please contact Berrett-Koehler:
Tel: (800) 929-2929; Fax: (802) 864-7626.

Orders by U.S. trade bookstores and wholesalers. Please contact Ingram Publisher Services, Tel: (800) 509-4887; Fax: (800) 838-1149;
E-mail: customer.service@ingrampublisherservices.com; or visit www.ingrampublisherservices.com/Ordering for details about electronic ordering.

Berrett-Koehler and the BK logo are registered trademarks of Berrett-Koehler Publishers, Inc.

Printed in the United States of America

Berrett-Koehler books are printed on long-lasting acid-free paper. When it is available, we choose paper that has been manufactured by environmentally responsible processes. These may include using trees grown in sustainable forests, incorporating recycled paper, minimizing chlorine in bleaching, or recycling the energy produced at the paper mill.

Library of Congress Cataloging-in-Publication Data
Rosenstein, Bruce.
    Living in more than one world : how Peter Drucker's wisdom can inspire and transform your life / Bruce Rosenstein. — 1st ed.
      p. cm.
    Includes bibliographical references and index.
    ISBN 978-1-57675-968-4 (hbk. : alk. paper)
      1. Quality of work life. 2. Quality of life. 3. Self-culture. 4. Interest (Psychology) 5. Drucker, Peter F. (Peter Ferdinand), 1909–2005. I. Title.
    HD6955.R68 2009
    650.1—dc22   2009018209

FIRST EDITION
14 13 12 11 10 09   10 9 8 7 6 5 4 3 2 1

Text design by Tag Savage at Wilsted & Taylor Publishing Services

To Deborah

This book would not exist without you.

CONTENTS

As I write this, the world is undergoing unprecedented social and economic upheavals. We need all the hope and good counsel we can get. It is just the time when we need the voice of Peter Drucker, and he is no longer here to speak to us.

So the timing of Bruce Rosenstein's *Living in More Than One World: How Peter Drucker's Wisdom Can Inspire and Transform Your Life* is fortuitous, and not just because it will be published in Drucker's centenary year. Rosenstein has distilled Peter Drucker's philosophy and teachings in a powerful way to help us meet new challenges and help others do the same. He brings the authentic Drucker voice to each reader.

The Peter Drucker I encounter in these pages is the man I met in 1981 and worked with while I was with the Girl Scouts of the USA. In 1990 I left the Girl Scouts and six weeks later found myself CEO of the new Peter F. Drucker Foundation for Nonprofit Management, now the

Leader to Leader Institute. He is wise but tough-minded. He is good-humored yet serious, and profound when the need arises. He is capable of introspection, yet always his focus is on others.

Readers who treat this book as an interactive experience will gain the most from it. In particular, Rosenstein's thought-provoking questions that you are encouraged to ask yourself throughout the text are reminiscent of Peter's consulting style: many questions—even seemingly obvious ones—to make your companion think about the reasons for a situation that is happening, and what that person can do about it. As you read this book, you may find yourself responding in the spirit of Drucker by thinking through your answers from every possible angle and questioning your own assumptions. You will move internally to ultimately have an external impact. Positive change beyond your own four walls will happen because of the change and growth within you, with the aid of this remarkable partner for the journey.

There are good reasons why a steady stream of articles, books, and Web sites continue to reference or quote from Drucker's words and work. He mastered the art of remaining relevant throughout a long lifetime. His followers have the satisfaction of knowing that his relevance has grown, expanding globally in the years since his death.

In a way that few authors have accomplished, Rosenstein's interviews draw out Drucker's wisdom in this intense, ongoing study of Peter Drucker as a person. Published over more than a decade, Rosenstein's many articles and interviews—appearing mainly in *USA Today*, but also in the journal *Leader to Leader* and elsewhere—demonstrate a keen perception of what continues to make Drucker so significant. Rosenstein extends that deep study and analysis into the pages of this book. He has interviewed not just Drucker himself, but also many of Drucker's friends, colleagues, and students. This book does not simply present Drucker's thinking, but takes a fresh approach by placing it in the context of how we can improve our lives now and in the future.

The answer, Rosenstein discovered, is to diversify our daily existence, much as Drucker himself did. It is to sharpen our sense of curiosity, remain open to new ideas, and learn as much as possible for as long as we can. It is to teach others, partly so we can learn more and be more effective. It is to be introspective when needed, but to remember that the most important things happen in the outside world. An especially important theme of our guidebook is generosity. We will be asked to share our time, talents, and expertise.

A successful diversification also involves doing what needs to be done today so that your future will be bright— the kind of future that will not unfold just because we or someone else predicted it. The book will provide many suggestions and strategies. You will find that a premium is placed on areas such as character, competence, achievement, and leaving something of value behind for others. These are presented not as a choice, but as essential. Rosenstein also reminds us that we must be aware of possible pitfalls in our diversification, including finding the time to do everything we want to do. Getting the most out of our reading will require ongoing work and thought, not a quick fix. Answers will emerge, but not because we have taken shortcuts. I believe Drucker would have appreciated that the entire book involves helpful action. You can start right now to make a better life for yourself and others, including people you will never meet, possibly those who may be born after your lifetime.

I have been deeply impressed since I first met Bruce Rosenstein by his rapport with Peter Drucker, which makes him as an author an especially companionable fellow traveler. Rosenstein writes from the viewpoint of a person facing the same challenges as his readers, with a fluid writing style that makes it easy for us to absorb the message.

It is not necessary to have ever heard of Peter Drucker, much less to have read his books, to enjoy and find value in *Living in More Than One World*. It is entirely possible that, beyond what you learn here, your curiosity will be stimulated to discover or return to Drucker's books. The suggested reading section at the end of this book will guide you to a select group of his most important books for individual development and personal growth. I believe you will now read or re-read these books with new eyes and a deeper appreciation of the meaning and philosophy of the Drucker message.

You will find it energizing to read and interact with the distilled, yet information-filled pages ahead. It will not be a passive experience. You will be elated as you discover that life and work approached with the Drucker spirit is a gift you can give to yourself, a gift that brightens the journey.

Frances Hesselbein
Chairman and Founding President,
Leader to Leader Institute
(formerly The Peter F. Drucker Foundation
for Nonprofit Management)

Chances are that you are part of the most crucial group of people in modern society: knowledge workers. Rather than earning your living by the sweat of your brow, your work revolves around what you know and can learn, making you the owner of your means of production. This distinction was drawn by Peter Drucker, the prolific author who was often called the father of modern management, in the late 1950s. Your knowledge is portable and not dependent on any particular employer or industry, and you are not limited geographically in where you do your work.

Today, life as a knowledge worker is more challenging than ever. Drucker's life and thought anticipated exactly the "flat world" described in Thomas L. Friedman's book *The World Is Flat* of zero job security, information overload, and 24/7 work expectations. As technology and education are spread and democratized, more people in more places become competition for the work you do.

This book will guide you on a personal journey of considering life holistically, based on the teaching and personal example of Drucker, who lived a fulfilling and productive life until his death at ninety-five in 2005. When you live in a holistic manner, you take a broad, inclusive view of everything and everyone that is a part of your life. You literally "live in more than one world," as Drucker told me during an interview before he died. That way, if you have setbacks in one area (particularly your work), you can bounce back more easily because you have other areas of strength and support.

This is particularly true in challenging economic times, with rampant unemployment, lost homes, and once-solid companies going bankrupt. If we place too much of our self-worth on a job that we lose, there is more damage than if we've built a strong support system and network.

The organizing theme of this book is creating and living a "total life" that includes your work, friends, family, professional colleagues, and affiliation groups. In this way, you can consider all of the elements of your life together and think of how each affects the others, now and in the future. To help accomplish this, you'll create and build a "Total Life List" as you read the book, or perhaps after you finish, if you're more comfortable doing it that way. Each chapter provides suggestions and background for working on your list. Your completed list (a living, changing document) will become one of the most valuable parts of your life, because it can tell you at a glance where you stand and where you'd like to go.

We'll consider both the advantages and, in some cases, the challenges or disadvantages of living a multidimensional life beyond the boundaries of your daily employment. The benefits of this type of life are that you can not only cushion the blows of setbacks such as the loss of a job or the bankruptcy of your company, but that you can meet and interact with people from other organizations and other walks of life. What you learn from these people and activities can be put to use in other areas of your life. Some possible disadvantages are that you may spread yourself too thin among your various activities and that you may find it difficult to find the time for the additional people in your life.

You will be given an uncomplicated framework and organizing principle for thinking about the benefits of living a total life and the challenges for today's knowledge worker. I am writing as a representative of that class of person. I worked as a librarian and researcher at *USA Today* for twenty-one years, until the final stages of this book. I also wrote for the Money section of *USA Today* for twelve years, and am a lecturer at the Catholic University of America's School of Library and Information Science. In the pages of this book, you'll consider life holistically in a way that goes beyond time management, career planning, or work-life balance.

You may wonder: "Wasn't Drucker known primarily as an author of books on management and as an adviser to *Fortune* 500 companies? Why is he relevant to my personal life?" Drucker also wrote about individual self-development and self-management. But these aspects of his thought are scattered across a number of his books and articles. In this book, I collect and synthesize his best lessons for knowledge workers into a logical structure. For you, the reader, this book is the self-help guide Drucker never wrote, and the next-best thing to being mentored by him.

Drucker's life can be a guide and inspiration for all

knowledge workers. For many years, he carried out an interrelated, multidimensional life. He taught at a school named for him, The Peter F. Drucker and Masatoshi Ito Graduate School of Management at Claremont Graduate University, in Claremont, California. He wrote bestselling books for nearly seventy years. He was a highly sought consultant both to corporations such as General Electric and Procter & Gamble, as well as to nonprofits such as The American Red Cross and the Girl Scouts of the USA.

Personal Study of Peter Drucker

I began to study Peter Drucker's ideas seriously in 1986, when his 839-page tome *Management: Tasks, Responsibilities, Practices* was assigned as the textbook for the management course I was taking at the Catholic University of America's School of Library and Information Science. That introduction launched my self-study of Drucker's work and of business and management books by other authors that continues to this day. I wrote about these books and interviewed authors for *USA Today* beginning in 1996, an undertaking that not only has been enjoyable, but also has provided me with an education in an important subject.

I interviewed and wrote about Drucker extensively for *USA Today* and other publications for more than a decade. In 2002, not long after interviewing him in Los Angeles for a feature story in *USA Today*, I decided to write a book on how knowledge workers could best apply his lessons for self-development and personal growth. It was an area of Drucker's work that I had long thought fascinating, yet that had not been thoroughly explored in books before, either by him or by other authors.

My research for this book included several interviews with Drucker and interviews with his former associates, such as colleagues, students, and consulting partners. My most important interview with Drucker was conducted on April 11, 2005, in Claremont, California, seven months to the day before he died. This interview—one of the last he gave—was videotaped. It is a revealing look at the wisdom of a ninety-five-year-old man who was still brimming with personal warmth and a sense of humor. You will have the opportunity to view the trailer of this interview on the Web at www.brucerosenstein.com, and I will continue to make presentations in as many cities as possible, based on both the book and the DVD.

I have also consulted material in the Drucker Archives at Claremont, and bring to this work the considerable background matter I have collected relating to Drucker and knowledge work for more than twenty years. You can now access much of the material I saw in person at the archives, which has been digitized and made available for free at www.druckerinstitute.com.

Chapter Overviews

Chapter 1, "Designing Your Total Life," lays out the concept of living in more than one world, the idea of having a multidimensional life that is not overly dependent on any one component. You'll begin work on your personal Total Life List, and continue throughout the book (and ideally after that!). We will also look more closely at the concept of the knowledge worker, and learn more about Drucker's life.

Chapter 2, "Developing Your Core Competencies," revolves around the idea of identifying and getting the most out of your personal areas of excellence. Although Drucker and others usually refer to this concept in the organizational sense, we will use it from the standpoint of the individual.

Chapter 3, "Creating Your Future," looks at how parallel and second careers prepare you for further journeys in life. It begins with the following Drucker quotation: "The purpose of the work on making the future is not to decide what should be done tomorrow, but what should be done today to have a tomorrow."

Chapter 4, "Exercising Your Generosity," explores some specific ways that you can make a positive difference in the lives of other people, through a variety of activities. We'll examine possibilities in volunteerism, mentorship, nonprofit organizations, and social entrepreneurship.

Chapter 5, "Teaching and Learning," revolves around the twin concepts at the heart of Drucker's success. He had a long-standing teaching career that was an integral part of his life. We'll look at your opportunities to become involved as a teacher, at the idea of continuous, lifelong learning—including Drucker's personal three-year self-study system—and also at the idea of learning how to learn.

The Conclusion, "Launching Your Journey," wraps up your personal journey in reading the book and helps you consider the implications for your own life. You will have thought about what you want to add (and subtract) from your Total Life List, and you can think of as many ways as possible to use the list as a personal, ongoing guide for your own inspiration and transformation.

"Suggested Readings" is a brief section that guides you to some of Drucker's most important books, with an emphasis on what you can learn from each about personal and professional development.

The Organization of the Book

Within each chapter, each section begins with a quote from Drucker that sets the stage in his own words. These snippets may lead you to investigate more of his writing. An amplification and contextual discussion follows each quote. Where appropriate, there are suggestions about ways to take advantage of a particular concept and put it into practice. In a similar fashion, you will be shown possible disadvantages and challenges to carrying out a concept. Each chapter section has a sidebar titled "Ask Yourself," with a couple of brief questions to get you thinking in a more personal way about the section topic, how it applies to you, and how it relates to your personal experience. Sidebars titled "Drucker's Life and Work" discuss how these concepts played out for Drucker himself.

Each chapter ends with a summary of the chapter's questions, a brief recap of the main points, and suggested activities that will help you build your own personal Total Life List. These activities are designed to get you thinking in a focused manner about your life both as it is now and where you'd like it to go. They provide a good complement to making the list, because they'll stimulate you to think about how you got to where you are in life and what you want for the future.

When you finish reading this book, you'll have learned not only how Peter Drucker lived a life of many dimensions, but how you can as well. Some readers will already be living along these lines, and the framework in these pages will help strengthen and deepen those dimensions, and aid you in making them connect with each other.

Drucker did not live long enough to see this book published. But I like to think that he would consider it to be a valuable extension of his legacy, and something of value for all knowledge workers. Perhaps, if he could magically read this now, he would reflect on what he taught and wrote, and how it continues to influence the lives of others, and consider that even he had learned something new.

Bruce Rosenstein
Rockville, Maryland, January 2009

ONE

Designing Your Total Life

The—I wouldn't say happy people but satisfied, contented— people I knew were more people that lived in more than one world. Those single-minded people—you meet them most in politics—in the end are very unhappy people.[1]

O n the morning of April 11, 2005, seven months to the day before he died at the age of ninety-five, Peter Drucker told me something that riveted me. I was interviewing him in Claremont, California, on the campus of the Peter F. Drucker and Masatoshi Ito Graduate School of Management at Claremont Graduate University. With cameras whirring in the background, we videotaped the interview. As I listened to his responses, the phrase "total life" popped into my head. I remarked to him: "What I think I'm hearing from you, at least partially, is that one needs to look at one's total life, one's family, friends, one's various organizations, and perhaps not be too focused on any one thing."

It was then that he gave me the answer, quoted above,

that became the cornerstone of this book. He added that there is little room at the pinnacle, and it is difficult to last long at the top. The answer is to spread out your time and talents on more than one activity, and to live and work among different groups of people, so that you are not overly reliant on any one thing for your happiness, sense of worth, and so on.

This seemingly simple idea has myriad implications. For example, if you have a setback in one area it won't destroy you. But the idea goes deeper. By living in more than one world, you constantly meet different people who can enrich your life. You learn more about how other people think, live, and work. You can gain different insights into yourself as a person. You become a more multidimensional person who is not overly dependent on any one particular area of life. You consider life not as a series of compartments, but as an ongoing series of activities, achievements, and commitments that give you a sense of meaning and fulfillment.

Peter Drucker drew strength, energy, and a sense of fulfillment from his three-pronged career: writing, teaching, and consulting. He had a wide circle of friends and professional contacts worldwide. He was a valued mentor to many former students and others. He wrote about and consulted for organizations in both the business and nonprofit worlds. The example of his work and life make him a great role model for today's knowledge workers, who feel overworked and out of control. In this chapter, we'll consider some the benefits and challenges of living in more than one world, and look at some of Drucker's bedrock principles that will help us lead more multifaceted lives.

The Knowledge Worker

No one but the knowledge workers themselves can come to grips with the question of what in work, job performance, social status, and pride constitutes the personal satisfaction that makes a knowledge worker feel that she contributes, performs, serves her values, and fulfills herself.[2]

IN THE LATE 1950S, toward the end of the Eisenhower era and before the profound changes in society of the 1960s, Drucker identified a new class—the knowledge worker—which he defined as people who work with what they know and can learn and who thus own and control their own means of production. Their knowledge is portable and not dependent on any particular employer or industry.

He saw the coming shift away from manual or unskilled work to the type of work we do more with our brains than our hands. He had the foresight to see ahead of time the often-painful changes in the economy as it moved from a dependence on manufacturing jobs to knowledge-based work. He alluded to this change in making a reference to his 1946 book *Concept of the Corporation*, which was based on an intimate, two-year look at the inside activities of General Motors: "The automobile factory, which I knew and studied during World War II and shortly afterwards, is gone. That today is a number of computerized work stations."[3]

Some contemporary examples of knowledge workers are people in the computer and information technology industries, teachers, doctors and other health-care professionals, scientists, lawyers, librarians, clergy, and people who work in the media. The concept of the knowledge worker is a powerful one, because it isn't tied to one definition or one group of people. The work of all people in this category has become even more crucial since Drucker articulated the concept, long before the era of personal computers, the Internet, and the World Wide Web.

Although managers were the ostensible audience for most of his books, Drucker had a following beyond management, and his work and ideas are too important to be appreciated only by managers. The 2008 publication of his *Management: Revised Edition* (the update of the "bible" of his books, *Management: Tasks, Responsibilities, Practices*, originally published in 1973) showed an emphasis on the individual knowledge worker that had been absent from the original book. The last part of the book is entitled "New Demands on the Individual," beginning with the chapter "Managing Oneself."

ASK YOURSELF

What knowledge do I apply to work? If I work in more than one job, do I apply different knowledge to each?

Beginning with his first book, *The End of Economic Man*, in 1939, and continuing for the next three decades, Drucker in his books focused more on business organizations and societal issues than individuals; the major exception was his classic from 1967, *The Effective Executive*. Even this had a business orientation, with an emphasis on how executives could run organizations not just efficiently but effectively. Doing the wrong thing efficiently is counterproductive. Yet beginning with *The Age of Discontinuity* in 1969, more space in his books was explicitly given over to the development of the individual as he began to flesh out the concept of the knowledge worker. In that book, he

One reason Drucker's ideas resonate so powerfully for knowledge workers is that he is a perfect prototype of the species. For many years, he lived a complex life, juggling multiple careers as a successful teacher, writer, and consultant, and made it work. He thought through his own contributions, and said it was important for his readers to be thoughtful about their own lives. His writing evolved, and he kept up with world events and remained relevant and sought-after deep into old age. He wrote not just about management, for which he is best known, but about society in general.

writes, "Today the center is the knowledge worker, the man or woman who applies to productive work ideas, concepts, and information rather than manual skill or brawn."[4] At the time it was first published, many more people were going to college and computers were becoming more sophisticated. The seeds of the Internet were planted in the same year the book was published. Microsoft was formed not long after, in 1975, and the early years of personal computers helped further the concept of the knowledge worker. Today it is difficult to think back to the late 1960s and see just how radical this idea really was.

Peter Drucker's Extraordinary Life

> Here I am, 58, and I still don't know what I am going to do when I grow up. My children and their spouses think I am kidding when I say that, but I am not. Nobody tells them that life is not that categorized.[5]

WE CAN'T IMITATE THE details of Peter Drucker's extraordinary life, but we can be guided by them. The outlines of his personal story are fascinating yet daunting. He and his wife, Doris Drucker—a remarkable person whom we'll meet later in this book—were married for sixty-eight years, with four children and six grandchildren. He published more than forty books and hundreds of newspaper, magazine, and journal articles. He was a longtime columnist for the *Wall Street Journal,* and often contributed to such prestigious publications as the *Atlantic Monthly* and the *Harvard Business Review.* In 2002, President George W. Bush awarded him the Presidential Medal of Freedom, the nation's highest civilian honor.

From 1971 until his death in 2005, he taught at the Peter F. Drucker and Masatoshi Ito Graduate School of Management at Claremont Graduate University, in Claremont, California, although he stopped teaching formal classes in 2002. The school was named after him in 1987, and the name of Ito, a major benefactor and admirer of Drucker, was added in 2004. As mentioned in the preface, Drucker was an in-demand consultant for both corporations and nonprofit organizations.

ASK YOURSELF

What patterns do I see in the outlines of Drucker's life? How could I apply any of them to my own life now, or soon?

In these details, we can see the outlines of what made him so successful, and how we can emulate him. He built variety into his life by working with different types of organizations and people. His distinct worlds complemented one another, so that what he learned in one area he could apply in another. His experience in working with organi-

Drucker kept in contact with many of his former students long after they graduated. Many phoned or visited him, and many more saw him at Founder's Day, the alumni gathering each November at the Drucker-Ito School. Until the final years of his life, he would randomly pick names of former students and call them to see how they were doing. He also asked them if, in retrospect, the school had been effective in their education.

zations would inevitably find its way into the pages of his books and articles. Drucker had a wide range of friends from the worlds of business, nonprofits, academia, and the arts. There is nothing stopping us from cultivating a similar group of talented and diverse people who are a regular part of our lives.

Multiple Worlds, and Beginning Your Total Life List

> *What matters is that the knowledge worker, by the time he or she reaches middle age, has developed and nourished a human being rather than a tax accountant or a hydraulic engineer. Otherwise, a few years later, tax accounting or hydraulic engineering will become awfully stale and boring.*[6]

SELF-DEVELOPMENT IS AN IMPORTANT theme in Drucker's books, even if it's not the one for which he is best known. When he advised managers, he was careful to say that the individual manager must develop as a whole person, and the same goes for the people he or she manages. In the upcoming chapters of this book we'll consider what constitutes your core competencies—the things you do with a sense of excellence and workmanship—that represent the best of what's inside you. We'll also explore what other activities fit in with this core sense of excellence. This means possibly finding a parallel career to what you are now doing, a type of work that may one day become your new core. We'll also look at the importance of continuous learning, which kept Drucker's mind active and alert for so many years.

ASK YOURSELF

Is there a mentor or a friend I could contact now who could give me ideas on how to add more multidimensionality to my life? Is there someone I could contact to offer assistance in defining life goals or priorities to explore new directions?

Closely allied to learning is the power of teaching. There are many benefits to adding teaching to the mix of your life. As Drucker said, you can learn a lot from your students besides what you teach them. A student has a unique personality and set of life experiences and skills that can be quite illuminating. As Drucker often pointed out, teaching something is often the best way to really learn a subject well. Teaching may well turn out to be an ideal parallel career, as well as a form of volunteerism—for instance, if you volunteer as a teacher in a church or other religious institution.

Another way to live in more than one world and increase your multidimensionality is through the concept of generosity. For many people, this means volunteering in nonprofit organizations. More people are also starting nonprofits, using skills they learned in a previous or parallel career, and becoming social entrepreneurs. For some people, generosity means becoming a servant leader, in either for-profit or nonprofit organizations. Servant leaders put the needs of their followers ahead of their own, and make sure that they have the tools to accomplish their mission. For still others, generosity means mentoring. Also key to living a holistic life is having serious outside interests that provide a sense of fun, enjoyment, and fulfillment.

To consider your total life, and figure out ways to develop a different, improved life, start by giving yourself an honest reality check of where things stand now. Begin by brainstorming to determine the sum total of your life, listing the people with whom you associate, and your various work and nonwork activities. You can also broaden it to include future goals and aspirations for people and activities in your life. "The effective people I know," Drucker said, "simply discipline themselves to have enough time for thinking."[7] This kind of self-assessment can be a challenge, but Drucker believed that thinking was hard work, which is why many people either devalued it or rarely did it seriously. We'll start on this at the end of this chapter in the exercise called "Hints for Creating Your Total Life

---

DRUCKER'S LIFE AND WORK

In Drucker's life, many of his outside interests, such as his appreciation of art and music and love of literature and history, found their way into his writing and teaching. He was a recognized expert on Japanese art, and taught this subject for several years at Pomona College while he was also teaching management.

List." It will be an ongoing activity throughout the book, and something you can continue creating long after you have finished reading.

The Benefit to Others

> *Knowledge workers therefore need to develop, preferably while they are still young, a noncompetitive life and community of their own, and some serious outside interest— be it working as a volunteer in the community, playing in the local orchestra, or taking an active part in a small town's local government.*[8]

LIVING IN MORE THAN one world can be an excellent strategy for many professionals. Consider each possibility in a variety of dimensions. Think continually of your options, while being mindful of possible pitfalls and drawbacks. This kind of life is rewarding, but it takes time and effort. There will inevitably be periods of frustration, but you'd have those anyway if you were living in just one world.

There are many advantages to adding other dimensions to your life. Drucker often pointed out that you could obtain leadership opportunities and experience that might not be available in your present job by volunteering in a nonprofit organization. You can combine leadership opportunities with work-related fulfillment by pursuing leadership positions within professional organi-

ASK YOURSELF

Who benefits from what I do in my work? Who are some other people I can serve in some way in my present job or through volunteer work?

The more worlds you inhabit, the more networking opportunities you have. The complementary nature of some of these worlds can be impressive. Drucker applied in one area, such as writing, what he learned in another, such as teaching or consulting. He considered his consulting practice to be a laboratory for his ideas. He met and interacted with different people depending on whether he was teaching, writing, or consulting. Though he maintained a select, limited number of consulting partners—many of whom remained close friends—he had a fresh crop of new students every semester for sixty years.

---

zations related to your work. If you have more than one dimension to your work with a parallel career, you have multiple chances for these kinds of positions. Professional organizations are often desperate for people who will take the lead in committees, annual conferences, and so on. You can develop yourself as a person and as a professional while giving back to your profession and helping others.

Drucker said that a key reason for seeking out more responsible positions in a nonprofit organization was the chance to be a more important person, whose work really mattered. This is important not just for the knowledge worker, but also for his or her family. It adds to a sense of self-worth and self-respect. Such work can also be more fulfilling than your daily job, because you can see the results of your labor more easily, and it aids a cause of your own choosing. Another important factor is that different sides of your personality and talents are elicited by the different dimensions in your life.

There are other tangible advantages to living in more than one world:

» You live more fully in the present while preparing for the future, but not being obsessed by it. By living in multiple dimensions, you'll have less time to ruminate on mistakes and regrets of the past, and you'll know that some of your actions are being taken to create your future life.

» By being multidimensional, you strengthen your sense of purpose, meaning, and fulfillment. You focus on spending time on activities and people that contribute to these areas.

» You deliberately choose activities that help make a positive difference in the lives of other people.

» And, as a bonus, you'll rarely be bored!

Drucker had a strong humanistic streak. By putting the spotlight on others, by showing his interest in them, by his concern for the outside world in all its forms, he made himself a better person throughout his life. These activities also helped keep him relevant until the end of his long life. His routine and sincere expressions of gratitude to others were also noteworthy. Most of us have many things for which to be thankful, and the people we encounter rarely receive the thanks that are often due.

The Challenges of Self-Management

In effect, managing oneself demands that each knowledge worker think and behave like a chief executive officer.[9]

THIS QUOTATION IS MORE than just a throwaway comment. If you think of yourself as CEO of your own life as a knowledge worker, you must make decisions and take actions based on more than what you think is best for you. Your thoughts must extend to the implications and effects on your colleagues, the organization itself and its stakeholders, as well as family and friends.

Drucker often claimed that self-management is a revolution in human affairs. He believed that history will show this revolution to be even more powerful than the changes brought on by technology—a powerful claim that can be judged only in retrospect. Until recent years, because of lack of mobility between and within jobs, and because of shorter life spans, self-management wasn't the necessity it has become. People live longer now, but organizations don't necessarily last as long as they once did.

But what did Drucker mean by self-management, and why is it relevant for living in more than one world? Drucker saw this as a self-directed, ongoing area, much as the management of an organization is ongoing and all-pervasive. Above all, it requires self-knowledge and a certain degree of introspection. In his major statement on this theme, the chapter "Managing Oneself" in the 1999 book *Management Challenges for the 21st Century*, Drucker presented these areas as crucial to managing yourself:

1. Self-knowledge regarding your values, strengths, and work habits
2. Finding where you belong in an organization, and which organization is right for you
3. Deciding on what you will contribute to your work and to the world
4. Taking responsibility for relationships
5. Planning for the second half of your life[10]

The prospect of managing yourself and living in more than one world can be daunting. For many people, it can become a goal or aspiration, rather than something to do immediately. Think of it as something to work toward, or to do incrementally. There are pitfalls to consider: You could possibly spread yourself too thin, and not give enough attention to an important aspect of life. You may make more money, but it's possible you'll make less if you don't concentrate 100 percent on one job or career. While it's wonderful to get to know new people in your various worlds, that means more people are competing for your time and attention. One of the most serious potential drawbacks is a possible inability to find the necessary time to work on your various activities because of the competing demands of each area.

ASK YOURSELF

Will I dilute my strength if I develop new parallel careers, or additional outside interests or activities? Have I ever had something in my life that I wanted to do for a long time, but that didn't work out the way I wanted it to? If so, what can I learn from the experience?

It is worth remembering that the one world in which none of us lives now or will in the future is a perfect or ideal world. We often have to make the most of what we have while we still have it. If we're waiting for the perfect time to start a new venture, or add new people to our lives, it is not likely to happen. It's better to take advantage of an imperfect world in aiding our personal transformations.

Sometimes new dimensions of one's life do not work out as planned. This happened to Drucker, who had a longtime desire to write novels. Two were published when he was in his seventies: *The Last of All Possible Worlds* (1982) and *The Temptation to Do Good* (1984). Both had tepid sales and indifferent reviews, and are now out of print. During an interview at his home in Claremont in 2003, I asked if he would decide to write novels again. His poignant reply: "It decided; I had no idea. I lived with the characters of those two novels for many years before I wrote the novels. I don't live with any characters [now]."[11]

Your Outside Interests

"Loafing" is easy, but "leisure" is difficult.[12]

GETTING THE MOST OUT of your nonwork time can be challenging. It's too tempting and easy to spend the hours away from the job passively. One of the things that contributed to Drucker's extreme longevity and continuing relevance was the fact that he was so well-rounded, with outside interests that he was able to incorporate when necessary into his work. Drucker knew that having serious interests beyond your job that also provide a sense of fun is a key aspect of living in more than one world.

In his own life, many of these outside interests, such as his appreciation of art and music and his love of literature and history, found their way into his writing and teaching. Whether or not you are able to draw on outside interests in your job, they are important as a way of delineating your time away from work. Diverse interests contribute to being well rounded and make you a more interesting person. They stimulate your creativity, which nourishes and enriches all areas of your life. There are many other areas in life where we can fulfill Drucker's idea of going beyond the world of work for personal development.

As important as work is, we put too much pressure on it to supply our complete sense of fulfillment. Other aspects of living, such as volunteering or teaching, provide further areas for fulfillment. In many cases the pleasure and sense of achievement afforded by outside interests may make all the difference in how happy we are, especially if work becomes a drudgery. Drucker noted how the expectation of satisfaction from work has both positive and negative connotations, because it's not always possible. Many people find that their outside interests dovetail well with their careers; for instance, drawing on their knowledge and love of music to take on a parallel career as a music teacher, or member of a band. Others who are talented in art may be able to show their artwork in local galleries.

In *Management Challenges for the 21st Century*, Drucker wrote that a key tenet of self-management is developing a second major interest in life, preferably early in your career. He distinguished between this type of serious interest and a hobby. He broadened this idea beyond just having outside interests to other areas, such as second or

ASK YOURSELF

What have I had to learn to get the most out of my leisure opportunities? Did it involve taking formal lessons or classes? Is there any nonwork area of my life in which I could be said to be a master or amateur expert?

parallel careers, or engaging in social ventures such as volunteerism or social entrepreneurship.

Beyond your daily employment, it is important to focus on things that may bring you pleasure, satisfaction, and a heightened sense of self-worth and growth, without their becoming a career. You engage in these activities for their own sake, even if they do have added benefits such as providing leadership experience. As Drucker so often said, all outside interests can provide a buffer against the inevitable setbacks and disappointments in life. They can provide you not only with a stimulating way of spending your time and a sense of fulfillment and satisfaction, but also a community of people distinct from your family and work colleagues.

As with other aspects of living in more than one world, meeting and interacting with new and different people is a cornerstone benefit. In *Managing the Non-Profit Organization: Practices and Principles*, Drucker wrote that it was "important, I think, for people who work in an organization to have an outside interest, to meet people and not just become totally absorbed in their own small world. And all worlds are small worlds."[13] In 1952, Drucker wrote "How to Be an Employee," a charming article based on an ideal but undelivered college commencement address, for *Fortune* magazine (it was later reprinted in the 1977 book *People and Performance: The Best of Peter Drucker on Management*). Besides containing valuable work and career advice couched in a highly accessible style, the article is remarkable for its focus on outside activities, given that it was written in the gray-flannel-suit, organization-man era. "But it is important in this 'employee society' of ours," he writes, "to have a genuine interest outside the job and to be serious about it."[14] Also notable is that it was writ-

Drucker integrated his outside interests into the fabric of his life. His love of reading, his extensive travels, and the study of history, literature, music, art, philosophy, and religion were expressed in his writing and his teaching. He was like a human hyperlink, referencing many disciplines within a single paragraph, and finding a way to tie them together so they made sense and conveyed his point.

Another way that Drucker integrated his outside interests with work carried over to his consulting. He was known to take clients on outings when they visited him in Claremont for consultations. Because Claremont is less than forty miles from Los Angeles, he was able to take advantage of a variety of settings for a combination of fun and education. If clients were there for several days, he might have taken them one day to a museum, another to a Los Angeles Dodgers baseball game, and one evening to the Los Angeles Philharmonic. This sense of cultural variety is something we can apply in our own lives, either on our own, or with friends, families, and colleagues.

ten well before Drucker identified the class of knowledge workers.

Since Drucker returned to this theme of outside activity off and on in books and articles for the rest of his life, it means that he wrote about this subject for more than fifty years. In the same 1952 article, he advocates doing something of your own choosing, with its own importance to you, where you "can be, if not a master, at least an amateur expert."[15] Some of his suggestions include studying local history, making music or furniture, and other pastimes.

The key thing is to pick something—or more than one thing—that interests you and that gives you pleasure and satisfaction. Some of these areas tap into material we will cover more fully in this book, such as teaching and learning in Chapter 5, and volunteerism in Chapter 4. For example, if one of your major outside interests is making music, chances are you will be engaged in some kind of ongoing training or study of it, and may be teaching or giving lessons for pleasure. The same goes for painting or drawing, sculpture, or other forms of art. If reading and writing are part of your interests, teaching and learning may be a crucial part of developing your interest and ability in both of these related areas.

Ideas that we will cover in upcoming chapters, such as time management and determining priorities (Chapter 2) and planning for the future (Chapter 3), will come into play in your pursuit of outside interests. One of the biggest obstacles is finding and making the time. If you are focused on your total life, and not too fixated on any one thing, it becomes easier to find and work with this discretionary time.

Maturity and Your Outside Interests

> *The person who will make the greatest contribution to a company is the mature person—and you cannot have maturity if you have no life or interest outside the job.*[16]

DRUCKER'S INTEREST IN MUSIC demonstrates how an outside interest can still have a strong impact on your main work. When describing management and career placement during an interview, Drucker illustrated his example with references to orchestra members playing Brahms. He likened the orchestra conductor to a manager. As we will discover in Chapter 2, the opera *Falstaff* by Verdi became a symbol for Drucker's lifelong quest for excellence and perfection.

In *The Effective Executive*, he uses Mozart to illustrate the dangers of multitasking. He says that Mozart was the exception among major composers, in that he could work simultaneously on different compositions and still turn out masterpieces. Bach and Handel, he says, could work on only one piece of music at a time. The lesson: "Executives can hardly assume," he writes, "that they are 'executive Mozarts.' "[17]

Drucker also stressed the importance of being a regular reader, no matter what subject matter you choose. He was a voracious reader, and his devotion to reading stood him in good stead throughout his life. It all comes down to asking: How are you going to spend your time and feed your mind? Drucker took pleasure in learning from the great minds of all ages, and it's an example anyone can follow. He was more likely to mention his reading of the Bible or novelists such as Jane Austen—one of his all-time favorites— than business books.

ASK YOURSELF

Are there similar analogies I can draw in my own life from the world of the arts, as Drucker did with his idea of "executive Mozarts"? Does my reading and experience of history, the arts, and other subjects dovetail with my main work, and, if so, in what specific ways?

One of Drucker's greatest outside interests was art. He was not an artist himself, but he studied, wrote about, and collected Japanese art, even teaching it at Pomona College, part of the Claremont schools. He and his wife of sixty-eight years, Doris Drucker, developed a major collection of Japanese art, the Sanso Collection, which has gone on traveling exhibitions. Drucker discovered Japanese art by a fluke: while working in London in June 1934, at the age of twenty-four, he ducked in out of a rainstorm to see a traveling exhibition of these paintings at Burlington Arcade. He stayed for two hours and became hooked for life.

He wrote this observation in a Japanese catalogue for the Sanso Collection: "Not only had I discovered a new universe of art. I had discovered something about myself; I had experienced a touch, a small touch to be sure but a genuine one, of enlightenment."[18] Drucker's introduction to an intense interest in Japanese life and culture became one of the hallmarks of his professional career. His interest was reciprocated by people in Japan, who have long been intensely interested in Drucker's work.

Keeping Active and Healthy

Only you can keep yourself healthy. That's new talk. It's old wisdom. Hippocrates said to drink only water from the spring, go to bed early, don't whore around, eat sparingly and nothing fat. People never listened to Mr. Hippocrates, because they were not paying a fee.[19]

EVEN INTO OLD AGE, Drucker maintained marvelous physical stamina. One of the reasons he gave for his longev-

ASK YOURSELF

What physical activities have refreshed and energized me in the past? What changes could I make to my daily and weekly routine to incorporate more physical activity, exercise, and wellness activities?

ity was the need to keep up with the pace set by his wife, Doris. She maintains a regular regimen of exercise and still plays tennis in her mid-nineties. She gave up hiking only in her early nineties. Regular exercise and taking care of your body are ways to get the most out of living in more than one world. If you're going to be multidimensional, you'll need energy and stamina not only for your work, but also for your outside pursuits. If you're feeling mentally or physically drained, you won't be able to focus your mind and body on the things you want to do. Fortunately, knowledge workers have many opportunities to nurture their health and strength. Some workplaces offer discounted or subsidized memberships to gyms. You can also take advantage of amateur sports opportunities. There are many classes and private teachers in such mind-body areas as yoga, meditation, and the Alexander Technique. The latter, though less well known, is helpful for a

DRUCKER'S LIFE AND WORK

Although Drucker tended not to give too much advice on how to maintain physical health and well-being, one of the reasons for his longevity was his exercise and active leisure pursuits. He was a regular swimmer who had a pool in his back yard and for many years, until his knees gave out, an avid walker and an active mountain hiker.

better, more productive use of your body through release of tension and improved posture. It has been particularly helpful to actors, singers, and musicians (you can learn more at www.alexandertechnique.com).

Chapter Question Summaries

The Knowledge Worker   Think about what knowledge you apply to work, especially if you have more than one job.

Peter Drucker's Extraordinary Life   Think about the patterns you perceive in Drucker's life, and how they might apply to your own.

Multiple Worlds, and Beginning Your Total Life List   Think about the people who can help you gain more multidimensionality in your life.

The Benefit to Others   Think about the people who benefit from your work, and how this can be spread to even more people.

The Challenges of Self-Management   Think about whether or not you'll dilute your strength by branching out into other areas of life, and whether setbacks in the past can be a valuable learning experience in the present.

Your Outside Interests   Think about what's involved in getting the most out of leisure opportunities, including whether or not you should take formal lessons or classes.

Maturity and Your Outside Interests Think about how Drucker incorporated his love and appreciation for literature and music into his life, and if there are or could be parallels in your own.

Keeping Active and Healthy Think about ways to change your routine to incorporate more physical activities and exercise, especially if your lack of stamina is hindering the possibility of taking on more dimensions in your life.

Chapter Recap and Next Steps

In this chapter we have laid the foundation for living a life of more than one dimension. We have covered:

» Drucker's concept of the knowledge worker, and who fits in that category
» How Peter Drucker's life can be a guide and inspiration for our own
» How self-development can be tied to living in multiple worlds
» Developing interests that also benefit other people, including the advantages of being multidimensional
» The definition of self-management, and why you should think of yourself as the CEO of your life
» How outside interests stimulate and nourish all areas of your life
» The importance of outside interests to your growth as a mature person
» The need for physical stamina and wellness to live your life to the fullest extent

In Chapter 2, "Developing Your Core Competencies," we will look at a toolbox of techniques to help you live more fully in more than one world. These include strengthening your sense of personal excellence and achievement, determining priorities, and the power of self-reflection.

Hints for Creating Your Total Life List

Drawing up your Total Life List will take some time, so think of it as an ongoing activity. If you are on social networking sites such as Facebook or LinkedIn, some of the work will have been done for you. Here is a framework to get you started and for your ongoing additions.

Sections of your list

1. Immediate family (current and future)
2. Extended family (current and future)
3. Closer work colleagues (people you interact with most often in the workplace)
4. Friends (current and future goals)
5. People in your various professional networks (current and future goals)
6. Various places of current employment and (briefly) what your work entails (current and future goals)
7. Professional affiliations and associations (current and future goals)
8. Ongoing learning activities (current and future goals)
9. Teaching (if any) (current and future goals)
10. Volunteer activities (current and future goals)

x with nonprofit organizations, or social entre-
eurship (current and future goals)
toring (current and future goals)
side interests of all types, including areas such as
sports leagues, amateur interest societies, religious/
spiritual activities or study, book groups, or creative
areas such as writing, art, or playing music (current
and future goals)
14. Exercise and other mind-body activities (current and
future goals)

As part of your future goals in some of the above categories, you may want to consider incorporating elements
from your past—people and/or activities—that were valuable for you and that you'd like to reintroduce in the future. This can be a way of reconnecting with old friends
or family members with whom you've lost touch, getting
back into activities that have been dropped, or possibly
looking into new educational opportunities at your alma
mater.

This list can be as specific, simple, or elaborate as you'd
like to make it. You can do it on paper or on computer.
Consulting the list as often as you like will give you a valuable snapshot of your life and will help you determine
areas in which you'd like to make changes or adjustments.
As you read this book, you'll have the opportunity to add
more items to your list.

A major difference between the list you create here and
what you may have done on Facebook or LinkedIn is the
fact that these items are not to be shared with the world
online, unless you choose to do so. The list is primarily an
aid to your personal self-development.

TWO

Developing Your Core Competencies

Leadership...rests on core competencies *that meld market or customer value with a special ability of the producer or supplier.*[20]

The concept of core competencies, originally developed at the organizational level, is increasingly being applied to individuals. Core competencies—what an organization can do better than others, or abilities that provide a particular competitive advantage—have been part of the business world's vocabulary since the phrase was introduced in the early 1990s. The term is associated with the authors Gary Hamel and C.K. Prahalad, first from their 1990 article "The Core Competencies of the Corporation" in the *Harvard Business Review*, and later in their book *Competing for the Future*.

While acknowledging the contributions of these authors and the idea of core competence, Drucker traced the principle back to his own work. In his 1995 book *Managing in a Time of Great Change*, Drucker said that organizations required "strengths analysis" (a term he coined in his 1964 book *Managing for Results*) to take advantage of opportunities. In the preface to *Competing for the Future*, Hamel and Prahalad pay tribute to Drucker, "whose wisdom has benefited our work enormously."[21]

For our purposes, the concept of core competence can be expanded to include the development of individual excellence. Such a focus can help you carry out the kind of life that leads to the highest achievement and personal satisfaction. Applying your competencies allows you to serve yourself as well as other people and society in general. Being really good at something—providing a high-quality service or product—has to be at the core of what you do, backed by a solid set of personal values.

What do you do so well that it gives you your best chance to contribute, at work and outside of it? Consider what is unique about what you do, and in what areas you excel. Some examples might be writing, communication, or selling. These are often abilities that can be applied to a variety of jobs or volunteer positions. Drucker said that, in his experience, few people could articulate their areas of strength. In this chapter, we'll look at a toolbox of techniques and concepts to help develop and strengthen your core competencies. They require work, thought, and concentration. Drucker cared deeply about his readers, but he didn't pamper them when offering his counsel. Sometimes you have to make tough, even painful decisions. For instance, in using the tool of systematic abandonment, which is discussed later in this chapter, you may find that as you regularly consult your Total Life List, you are not giving the proper time to activities within your core competencies. You will then need to make a decision on what other activities must be stopped.

Workmanship, Excellence, and Diligence

This is the first thing I have learned, during these fifty years of working with, and studying, institutions and the people who manage them: workmanship counts.... Few tasks in any discipline require genius. But all require conscientiousness.[22]

THE FIRST ITEMS IN your toolbox are workmanship, excellence, and diligence; these are bedrock qualities for getting the most out of your core competencies.

Drucker elaborated on the idea of workmanship during a speech he gave at the Claremont Graduate School (now Claremont Graduate University) when the management school was named after him, on October 21, 1987. In the speech, and eight years later in his book *Drucker on Asia*, he described the story of Phidias, "the greatest sculptor of ancient Greece," whose creations "still stand on the roof of the Parthenon in Athens."[23] As Drucker remembered the story, Phidias presented his bill to the Athenian accounting office, which protested having to pay for work on the back of the statues, which could not be seen by people on the ground. Phidias insisted that although people could not see the backs of the statue, the Gods could. At face value, this means that doing high-quality work is important even if it's not obvious to everyone. It doesn't mean charging for work that is not important. The big takeaway here is that you should develop inner standards of excellence that are high, yet attainable. You never know who is going to see and judge your work. It's best for all concerned if you've delivered something of the highest quality of which you are capable.

Drucker was considered a genius, but he was also hard-working, diligent, and determined, attributes that anyone can emulate. He approached his work in an enthusiastic, open-minded, and receptive way. He stressed the power of observation, attention to detail, and having a radar for determining what is most relevant about any given situation or piece of information. If you want to advertise or market your work, you must start from a basic level of, if not excellence, then at least very strong competence. People will only want your services if you can deliver on your promises. You can market cleverly all you want, but you're unlikely to have repeated, ongoing calls for your services or products if people are disappointed by the quality of your work.

ASK YOURSELF

Considering Drucker's example of Phidias and his statues, has a particular piece of workmanship inspired similar thoughts and admiration within me? Is there an equivalent to the Verdi opera experience, artistic or otherwise, in my life? What did I learn from it, and how did it change me?

Drucker strove not only for excellence, but also for the elusive goal of perfection. As we have seen, some of his personal self-management lessons came from his early life experiences. While he studied at Hamburg University in Germany, he attended the Hamburg Opera with low-priced student tickets. A performance of Verdi's *Falstaff* became a turning point in his life. He discovered the youthful-sounding opera had actually been written by the composer in his eighties. Drucker found out that Verdi had noted that although his lifelong pursuit of perfection always eluded him, he wanted to give it one more try.

Drucker was powered more by success in his life than by the redemption of failure. He never wrote fiction again after his two novels failed to succeed. "I've learned to run with success and not worry too much about non-success," he said. "You know there's an old saying 'At first if you don't succeed, try, try, try again.' It's wrong. If at first you don't succeed, try once more, and then try something else."[24] There is a fine line between persistence and futility. It is not to be thought of as an ironclad rule, since the third time may be the charm in some situations. But we all have to consider how much time and effort we put into something before we realize it's not working and that the time has come to move on.

Drucker later vowed that these words would give him a guiding principle for his own life, especially if he reached an advanced age.

Achievement

Achievement is addictive.... The achievement that motivates is doing exceptionally well what one is already good at.[25]

A SENSE OF ACHIEVEMENT is the next tool. Your core competencies allow you to work toward meaningful achievements. The sense of achievement can be most pronounced in the realm of work, and it helps to express who you really are as a person. "Work is an extension of personality," Drucker wrote. "It is achievement. It is one of the ways in which a person defines himself or herself, measures his or her worth and humanity."[26] You can periodically assess whether or not the work you are doing really is an extension of your personality. If it's not, you can consider strategies for changing jobs, or the type of work you do.

Of course, work is not the only way to measure your worth or humanity. A couple of other potential areas of self-worth are:

» Your sense of generosity, whether through volunteering, mentoring, or other forms of giving to others
» What you accomplish in your outside interests—perhaps an achievement in sports or music—that takes time and effort but has nothing to do with work

With proper care, achievement is open to anyone. Drucker's tough-love approach comes into play with the following assessment: "Whenever I hear executives complain about the reactionary organization they work for, about how nothing can be done, about how stupid the boss is, I feel tempted to tell them: 'Stop bellyaching about what you cannot do. What *can* you do?' "[27]

To get the most out of work and life, we would do well to follow Drucker's teaching and personal example of drawing on inner resources for accomplishment. "Knowledge workers," he has written, "except at the very lowest levels, are not productive under the spur of fear; only *self-motivation* and *self-direction* make them productive. They have to be *achieving* in order to produce at all."[28] There are many people who believe that management-by-fear is still too prevalent in our workplaces.

Drucker drew a distinction between achievement over a lifetime of good work versus the goal of making money for its own sake. "I've known quite a few people," he said, "whose main goal was to make money. And they all made it.... If you are single-minded, focused on making money, you'll make money. And without exception, they were all utterly miserable. They reached that goal, and there was nothing left."[29] The solution is to focus on what you do and the benefit it has not just for you, but for others. It doesn't mean that you won't make money—many of Drucker's followers are quite well off financially—but it does mean that the pursuit of money plays a subordinate role. "So, if your goal is to make money, I rather pity you," Drucker said. "The people I have seen who were happy even after being successful are the people who want to leave something behind. A hospital that's working, a company that's working, whatever, or who are not money-focused, but achievement-focused, because that you're never finished with."[30] If you lead a multidimensional life, you have to give enough thought to which areas—possibly built on your core competencies—you will give the most emphasis.

ASK YOURSELF

Do I give myself enough credit each day for the achievements I make, or do I take them for granted? What is a particular lesson learned from my early work experience that is so powerful that I will never forget it?

Drucker had a related concept that you might find handy when you have simultaneous competing tasks. Ask yourself what needs to be done rather than what you want to do. This can be applied not just to daily tasks, but to the larger areas of your life. There is often a discrepancy between what is easier or more pleasant to do, versus what

Drucker's time as a young journalist in Germany helped form his well-developed work ethic and informed his later work as an author. When he was twenty, in his first reporting assignment in Germany at the newspaper *Frankfurter General-Anzeiger*, he covered a criminal trial. When he returned from the court to write his story, the editor wanted to know the name of the prosecutor. Drucker hadn't found out this crucial detail, and was instructed to find out. He had to go to the man's home and wake him up to find out the name. Attention to detail, really paying attention to our life and work, is crucial. Drucker honed his powers of observation over the years. There is no reason that we can't follow his lead.

really needs to be tackled. If what needs to be done is not within your core competencies, you can make some decisions on how to proceed. Can someone else do it better, such as through delegating or outsourcing? Would some investigating and learning on your part help a task become part of your core competencies, and, if so, with how much additional effort?

The Effective Use of Time

> Learn to manage your time. The secret is not to do the five million things that do not need to be done and will never be missed.[31]

TIME MANAGEMENT IS AN important tool for leading a multidimensional life based on your core competencies.

In *The Effective Executive*, Drucker set out a valuable framework for keeping track of your time. He advocated that at work you should write down everything you do and how much time it takes, so you can see how you really spend your day, as opposed to how you think you spend it.

You can go beyond that by listing what you do at work and outside of it, with rough guidelines for how much time you are spending on each activity. This exercise works only if you are ruthlessly honest with yourself. If you find you're spending several hours each day watching television or doing something else you find too passive, you can then decide to make changes. Doris Drucker said that neither she nor her husband watched television. Not everyone might want to go that far, but at least it is something that can be considered in terms of time expended versus benefit derived.

ASK YOURSELF

Do I use a time management system now? Have I looked into systems in books like David Allen's Getting Things Done *or Stephen Covey's* The 7 Habits of Highly Effective People? *At first glance, what activities might I have to give up in order to take on new dimensions in my life?*

To lead a satisfying life in more than one world, you'll have to create the time to accomplish what you want. You'll have to give the proper hours to the proper activities. If you have one main job, you'll have to consider how you will carve out the remaining hours of each week to exercise your spirit of generosity, develop a second career, or pursue outside interests.

Drucker's output was prodigious, yet he was selective with his time. He could have responded to increasing numbers of opportunities. He could have taken more consulting assignments by creating an organization in his name. But then most of the work would not have been done by him, and he felt that he worked best on his own. In a similar manner, he could have hired research assistants and cranked out even more books and articles. But at some point he knew that quality would be diluted and his work would suffer. People would not be getting 100 percent Drucker anymore. As you apply time management in your own life, it doesn't mean you can't create an organization in your name, or hire people to help you. It does mean that you should think about how you can best express your talents and ideas, and how much you want to, or are able to, involve other people in the process.

Priorities

A decision therefore has to be made as to which tasks deserve priority and which are of less importance.[32]

WORKING ON ACHIEVEMENTS IS easier if you can prioritize your work and other aspects of your life. In 2005, Drucker said, "My order of priorities is: writing comes first, teaching next, and consulting last."[33] However, he gave slightly different answers at other times in his life. Three years earlier, he said, "If you want to diagram my work, in the center is writing, then comes consulting, then comes teaching. I've never been primarily an academic. I like to teach because that's the way I learn."[34] There is no rule about how often you should reevaluate your priorities. Periodically checking, adding to, and subtracting from your Total Life List will give you a better sense of where you stand, and where your priorities are at any given time.

Drucker listed his priorities for allocating his time, but that is only one part of priority setting. Another is how you handle your daily tasks. Taken together, setting priorities is a crucial activity for anyone living in more than one world. You have many different people and activities competing for your time. If you are unclear on your daily and long-range priorities, you can waste time on things that ultimately aren't that important or satisfying.

ASK YOURSELF

Have I ever considered the various areas of my life and then prioritized them as Drucker did? When was the last time I aimed high, at something that would make a difference, and what happened as a result?

In *The Effective Executive*, Drucker set out four rules for priority setting, which can be briefly summarized as:

1. Focus on the future, not the past.
2. Focus on opportunities, not problems.
3. Don't climb on bandwagons.
4. Forget safe options; aim high, at "something that will make a difference."[35]

These four rules dovetail with his overall message, that the future is based on today's actions and decisions, and that to have a satisfying future, you can't be overwhelmed by your problems, or let them take up an inordinate amount of your time and money.

Around the time that *The Daily Drucker* was published, Drucker said he developed a framework after finishing an assignment or project. Tapping into the power of self-questioning, he would first ask himself what needed to be done now, and the answer would lead to something new. He said that was not the difficult part; what was difficult was the next question: determining priorities. "That takes me quite awhile as a rule," he said, "and a lot of agonizing. But it has to be asked and has to be answered."[36] If someone of his achievements and stature felt that way, it should come as no surprise that the rest of us might have trouble dealing with setting priorities.

The Power of Self-Reflection

I think a more important lesson I've learned is that I need to look back every year on the results of the year and hold them against my expectations.[37]

SOMETIMES YOU NEED TO get away from the daily grind to focus on your core competencies and purpose in life. Many people find value in activities such as personal retreats, Sabbaths, and meditation. Daily activity is too hectic and pressured to do much planning and reflection. Drucker believed that thinking is hard work and it is devalued in our fast-paced society. The main value of a discipline like meditation is that it clears your mind to make it easier to consider what really matters in your life. Some people find similar values in yoga, walking, running, or spending time in nature.

Drucker said that other effective people he knew had

similar regimens, which they undertook away from the workplace and its distractions. Microsoft's Bill Gates has made profitable use of what he calls "think weeks," when he goes away for reading, reflection, and planning. The point is to have time built into your schedule to get away from work to think deeply about where you have been and where you are going.

Here are some ideal incremental steps for this inward journey:

ASK YOURSELF

Where and how could I get away from my daily responsibilities to begin engaging in self-reflection? How can this self-reflection relate to and help my annual performance review at work, where I am asked to review the accomplishments of the past year and plan my work goals for the next? How can it help me assess my personal goals?

» Assess the past year against the plans you made a year ago
» Decide what worked during the year and what didn't
» Try to determine where the opportunities are
» Based on this, map a plan for the coming year

Not all of us have the time or inclination to spend Drucker's suggested "week in the wilderness" to accomplish this planning. But we can all strive to carve out some time, in whatever season and whatever setting, for this self-reflection. Some people find benefit in periodic retreats, alone or with others. This type of retreat can, but doesn't have to be, spiritually based. However, this is similar to the idea of a Sabbath, taking a day each week to pause,

Drucker took time each summer to consider how the previous year had gone, and what he would do in the coming year. Long after he reached the top of his field and became famous, Drucker still took the time for these periodic self-examinations, which showed his diligence and lack of complacency. He said, "Every year I'm surprised. Every year the things that worked are not the things I expected to work. And the things I expected to work are at best not failures. And every year I redirect my priorities as a result of that test and a year later find out that I have not lived up to my priorities but have done something quite different. So, I have learned that one has to plan, but one doesn't follow the plan."[38] This kind of contemplation is a perfect example of the combination of action and reflection that helped make Drucker such a success in life.

to reflect, to aim for self-renewal, and to pay attention to the blessings in your life. The 24/7 nature of society makes it more difficult to do this, but many find it a nourishing discipline.

Your Legacy

> *When I was thirteen, I had an inspiring teacher of religion, who one day went right through the class of boys asking each one, "What do you want to be remembered for?"*[39]

HOW DO YOUR CORE competencies fit in with the question Drucker's teacher asked him long ago? The answer to this question isn't easy, and for many of us there will be more than one answer. Drucker has said that the answer will probably change as you grow older. The Drucker legacy, the achievement for which he will be remembered, lives on in his books and articles, and in the lives of the people he touched and influenced. It is further embodied in the teachings at the Drucker-Ito School, the Drucker Societies, and the Drucker Institute. For more on the latter two institutions, see Chapter 4.

If you wait to do quality work based on your core competencies, or put off thinking about your legacy, you may not get a chance to leave behind what you really feel is representative of the best of you as a person. None of us knows how long we will live, and time is rarely in adequate supply for all the things we want to do. We need to do everything possible to maximize whatever opportunities we have, whether they are in our present work, outside activities, or new opportunities we pursue because we judge they will be a better use of our time and talents.

I twice interviewed and wrote about Richard Carlson, author of the *Don't Sweat the Small Stuff* series of best-

---

DRUCKER'S LIFE AND WORK

Drucker wanted to be remembered as someone who provided insight and helped people reach meaningful goals. "None of my books or ideas mean anything to me in the long run," he told interviewer Harriet Rubin in *Inc.* magazine in 1998. "What are theories? Nothing. The only thing that matters is how you touch people. Have I given anyone insight? That's what I want to have done. Insight lasts; theories don't."[40] This is an extraordinary statement from someone who has sold millions of books. It may seem as though he is intentionally downplaying his achievements and being overly modest. He also seems to be talking about his direct encounters or relationships with people. But his books and theories have also helped to provide insight to people he never met, and to people far into the future who will continue to read his books.

---

selling self-help books, for *USA Today*. He had a special way of encapsulating highly relevant personal development advice for people in short, easily digestible bites. I found him to be a genuinely nice, thoughtful person, with important things to say. So I was stunned to read in December 2006 that he had died of a heart attack at the age of forty-five on an airplane, on the way from California to New York to promote his latest book.

Carlson's death was tragic, particularly because he left behind a wife and two young daughters. But in true Drucker fashion, he also left behind a number of books that many readers find helpful and useful. He also left behind for his readers a basic way of approaching life: living purposefully but not getting too stressed about things that are beyond our control. Carlson had an organization to carry on his work, starting with his Web site. It's safe to say that, despite his death, his benefit to people will continue for many years. If you want to do things that make you proud, and that will have lasting value for others, you must devote the proper care, thought, and effort each day. This sense of purpose, of knowing and believing in yourself, is a direct link to fulfillment and meaning.

ASK YOURSELF

What would my friends, family, and co-workers say my legacy is? Has an example similar to the one about Richard Carlson touched me in a particular way? What can I learn from that person's life and legacy?

Carlson was highly productive, regularly publishing books and a newspaper column. He couldn't have done that without an ongoing focus on the work that best expressed his talents. Think about it: Carlson lived fifty years less than Drucker. Under different circumstances, he might well have been as prolific over a long life as Drucker was. His sudden death at such a relatively young age proves that we can only count on what we do today to leave a legacy for tomorrow.

Values and Your Place in Life

People are effective because they say "no," not because they say "yes," because they say "this isn't for me."[41]

HOW DO YOU KNOW what opportunities are right for you? Especially in uncertain, challenging economic times, offers of jobs, projects, or investments may seem tempting, but ultimately not a good personal fit. "The unhappy people I've known," Drucker said, "are the ones who can't resist what looks like a big chance, a big promotion, a big success, that is not for them. Skills one can acquire, values no. And the people I've seen who are really unhappy are in a position where the values of the organization don't fit them."[42] None of us wants to be unhappy, especially if the source of this state of mind is a job to which we devote a third or more of our hours.

Drucker believed that underpinning your life, and implicit in everything you do, should be a bedrock sense of values, character, integrity, and a belief in ethics. Organizations, as the sum total of the people they employ, should also exhibit these characteristics. His idea that you can acquire skills but not values is a powerful and profound one. It cuts both ways: if you personally don't have the proper values, they can't be acquired. If your organization doesn't have them, it is not going to acquire those values just for you.

As far back as the early 1950s, years before he identified the species of knowledge workers, Drucker gave advice on how to be a valuable employee: "But fundamentally the one quality demanded of you will not be skill, knowledge, or talent, but character."[43] This belief was evident throughout his life and was a continuing theme in his books.

At some point, Drucker argued, you have to know when to strive, and know when to stop. He contrasted the fates of two friends. One became a successful politician, elected as both governor and senator. Drucker said he was "a very happy man. He didn't want to be President, the last thing he wanted to be. He loved to be senator." Another friend also became quite successful, reaching the pinnacle of his career in his early fifties. Drucker said this friend "spent another thirty years basically thirsting for more instead of enjoying, instead of saying, 'What can I do to make this really have an impact?'"[44] That can be a powerful question to ask yourself. It's the sort of question that can lead you to search for more dimensions in your life. If as part of your legacy you want to be remembered for helping other people reach their goals and potential, for example, teaching, mentoring, or volunteering may turn out to be more fruitful than what you do in your main job.

ASK YOURSELF

Has there been a time in my experience that I reached the top, but realized it was too difficult to stay there?

Have I asked myself how, in my present job, I can gain maximum impact from the work I do?

What can you do in your life, considering all its dimensions and possibilities, that will really make a difference and have a positive, lasting effect on the lives of others, or society in general? "Every few years," Drucker said, some people "try, consciously or not, something new. Others don't. Others when they find where they belong will never touch anything else. And I think that that also changes with age."[45] He reminded readers that you can be guided by opportunities and directives from your employer, but decisions central to your life and aspirations are your own responsibility.

In his consulting work, Drucker said he would pass on certain types of assignments, in which companies or organizations wanted him "to be a hatchet man, which I refused to do. I'm no good at it. I don't believe in it."[46] Drucker was in the fortunate position of being able to turn away work because he was so much in demand. Not

---

DRUCKER'S LIFE AND WORK

In his book *Management Challenges for the 21st Century*, Drucker relates a telling anecdote about how he handled a value conflict when he was a young man, and how it led to his eventual multidimensional life. He was working in a London bank as an asset manager and doing quite well. He was already focused on how to make his most meaningful contribution to the world, and he realized it wouldn't be doing that kind of work. He decided that his values lay in working with people. Despite the Depression and the lack of another job, he quit the job he had, which may have seemed like a foolhardy decision to others. He eventually immigrated to New York, where he began his career as a serious writer, followed in short order by teaching and consulting. How much would the world have missed had he not gone outside of his comfort zone and left the world of banking?

---

all of us will be in the same position. But we can still follow his lead and stay true to our values and not compromise our principles.

Systematic Abandonment

"If we did not do this already, would we, knowing what we now know, go into it?"[47]

AS YOU CONTINUE TO check your Total Life List on a regular basis, practice what Drucker called systematic abandonment (also known as planned or organized abandonment). Although this technique was designed to be practiced in organizations, it is valid for personal use. He advocated its use for individuals—although he didn't specifically use the term abandonment—in his 1990 book *Managing the Non-Profit Organization*. But like much of Drucker's advice, systematic abandonment is not easy. The idea is, at regular intervals of your choosing, to step back and consider all your activities. Substitute "I" for "we" in the quotation that opens this section, and apply it to every activity on your list. If your answer is that you wouldn't initiate a particular activity, decide if you should stop, and how you'll stop.

ASK YOURSELF

Does my workplace engage in anything like systematic abandonment? If so, how does the procedure work? If I ask myself right now whether I would keep doing all the activities I am now engaged in, is there anything obvious that I could eliminate immediately to make room for something better?

Although Drucker kept his basic framework of writing, teaching, and consulting for many years, he was judicious with his use of time. He did not take on activities, no matter how attractive, that would dilute his strength or detract from his daily expression of his core competencies. This meant turning down numerous offers to lecture, write forewords to books, and consult with organizations worldwide.

You may decide that certain activities clearly don't tap into your core competencies and what you enjoy doing. Systematic abandonment is also a wise use of time during your periods of self-reflection, because you are asking some of the big questions about your life, yourself, and your activities. These can be difficult things to tackle during a busy workday, or even after work, when you are probably still busy with other areas of your life. Practicing systematic abandonment may mean giving up—or spending less time at—things that have been successful, and activities that you enjoy. It could be that you want to make time in your life for new activities, such as teaching, learning, or volunteering, and in order to make time, something else will have to be cut or scaled back.

Chapter Question Summaries

Workmanship, Excellence, and Diligence Think about particular experiences similar to Drucker's response to the story about the Parthenon, and Verdi's opera *Falstaff*, that changed your life or way of thinking.

Achievement Think about your own approach to the concept of achievement, and whether you give yourself enough credit for what you achieve. Consider your early work years: are there powerful lessons to be drawn from those experiences that you haven't previously considered?

The Effective Use of Time Think about time management systems: if you are now using one, how valuable is it to you? If you're not using one, which one should you choose, and why?

Priorities Think about prioritizing the basic activities of your life, as Drucker did. Consider giving priority to an activity that aims high and makes a difference.

The Power of Self-Reflection Think about making time for periodic self-reflection and contemplation. Consider how you can incorporate what you learn into the self-assessment you perform during your annual performance review at work.

Your Legacy Think about what you'd like your own legacy to be. Consider the legacy of people you have admired, especially those who may have died at a relatively young age.

Values and Your Place in Life Think about what constitutes reaching the top of your organization and profession, and the difficulties not only of achieving that position, but also of staying there.

Systematic Abandonment If your workplace engages in this activity, how does it work? In your own life, look for activities that can be eliminated to make way for something more fruitful; aim to increase activities within your core competencies, or that would contribute to your legacy.

Chapter Recap and Next Steps

In this chapter we have seen how the development of your core competencies—the areas in which you really excel and make a difference—can be furthered by applying a number of Drucker's tools and techniques.

We have covered:

» How cultivating a sense of personal excellence through diligence and workmanship is more important than being a genius

» Why a sense of achievement is more important than having a goal of making money for its own sake

» Why you must be selective with the use of your time, beginning with knowing how you use it in the first place

» How to determine priorities by focusing on the future rather than the past and aiming high at something that will make a difference

» The importance of periodically getting away from your daily duties to reflect on how your year has gone, and what you will do differently in the future

» Why you should think about your legacy, what you want to be remembered for, as you go about your daily work

» How your personal values affect a successful and productive life and career, and how you will not be happy with a mismatch of values between you and your workplace

» Why you must systematically stop doing some things that have been successful and enjoyable, in order to make way for something even better in the future

In Chapter 3, "Creating Your Future," we'll look at how finding opportunities for parallel and second careers can lead to a better personal future. We are not trying to predict the future with a crystal ball, but are doing the work today that enables the future.

Hints for Creating Your Total Life List

Look at what you've included so far on your list. Think about how some of the Drucker-related concepts in this chapter, such as excellence, achievement, self-reflection, systematic abandonment, and others, are already affecting or could have an effect on each area in your life.

You may develop more ideas about adding (or subtracting) items in the list by beginning to schedule a comfortable length of time—a day, a weekend, or even a few hours—to try self-reflection. For a period of a week (or longer), each evening write down or keep a computer file of anything, even and especially small things, that contributed to your self-development and lessons learned. These can serve as a guide to what you're doing right, and can be inspirations for the future when you need an emotional lift.

Check online for opportunities for retreats, or classes on meditation or yoga. You might find value in writing about your experience, as either a form of journaling or a personal essay, to help find new insights into your life and work.

One way of interpreting Drucker's words, and the personal example he set, is to look back at the end of each day and find that you are in a higher intellectual, and even spiritual, place. The ideal is to achieve at least some measure of personal growth and fulfillment each day.

THREE

Creating Your Future

The purpose of the work on making the future is not to decide what should be done tomorrow, but what should be done today to have a tomorrow.[48]

Drucker was an advocate of looking out the window for "the future that has already happened." One of his most-quoted metaphors, it is open to many interpretations. As we seek to live in more than one world and build and maintain a life that has several dimensions, we can determine ways to remain rooted in the present while keeping an eye on the future for how we will diversify our time and talents. It is important to be aware of the Drucker-like qualities of being observant, endlessly curious, and open-minded.

In this chapter we'll explore how to prepare for the future while not neglecting the present. You can prepare for the work and other activities of the future by taking steps now, such as planning for parallel and second careers. If you are under forty, you can begin thinking about the second half of your life. For those over forty, it's never too late to shift into parallel or second careers. Some of these moves may cause significant enough changes that you will reinvent yourself, something that Drucker advocated in his book *Drucker on Asia*.

Underpinning all of this planning and activity is the idea that the knowledge and skills of a knowledge worker are portable and mobile. Unlike manual workers, you have numerous options on where, how, and for whom you will put your knowledge to work. As Drucker so often noted, this is a fairly recent phenomenon, and many people have not yet come to grips with its implications for the present or the future. The technology that aids this portability continues to outstrip even what Drucker considered. Although he had a good intuitive grasp of what computers could do from observation, study, and working with people in the computer industry, he was not a computer user himself. This means that you will have advantages that he did not, since your experience with software and databases is firsthand and probably fairly sophisticated.

Drucker is often quoted as saying that the best way to predict the future is to create it. He had little time for futurists or for predictions about the future, because he thought such predictions were futile. You only know what you can do, what you can aim for, and what you can extrapolate from the present. You can look at current trends and decide what their implications are, if any, for the future. Then you can decide what your place might be in that future. What are current trends that affect your daily life? How do you think they will affect your future? What can you do to ensure that their impact will be positive?

One of the best ways to start making the future is to begin the kind of life diversification that is central to this book. You can use the kinds of skills and knowledge related to your core competencies discussed in Chapter 2 to begin thinking about parallel or second careers, and how they might fit into the second half of your life.

The Second Half of Your Life

For the first time in human history, individuals can expect to outlive organizations. This creates a totally new challenge: What to do with the second half of one's life?[49]

AS NOTED IN CHAPTER 1, Drucker said preparation for the second half of life is one of the key tenets of self-management. It can also be one of the most difficult, because it challenges our current thinking and ways of doing things. It means planning for and going into the unknown. It means the possibility of failure, at least at first.

Not only do we have the challenge of outliving our organizations, but we are also living longer than our ancestors did. We are fortunate that because we have not done the hard physical labor of manual workers, we are not physically worn out during the second half of life. We may, however, be mentally and spiritually drained, bored, or burned out by midlife. Drucker wrote that the fabled midlife crisis of executives was mostly boredom. Although he wrote of people becoming so bored and jaded that they had, in essence, retired on the job, that is a less common phenomenon today. Some people still may "retire on the job," but there are fewer occasions for that to happen in today's shrinking workforce. Many people (especially those over age fifty) are being eased out of jobs long before this kind of crisis sets in. Others are increasingly vulnerable to job elimination through outsourcing or offshoring. These factors make planning for a second career even more imperative.

These are all reasons, Drucker advised, that we should think of making changes in what we do and how we do it. Because we are able to approach these decisions from a more mature, experienced standpoint than we could earlier in life, we may seek to find and create more meaning for ourselves and others.

For guidance on charting the second half of one's life, Drucker recommended the books by his longtime friend and associate Bob Buford, who is now the chairman of the Drucker Institute. Buford has written about and also successfully planned and carried out a different and no less productive second half of life. Drucker wrote the forewords to two of Buford's books: *Halftime: Changing Your Game Plan from Success to Significance* (1994) and *Stuck in Halftime: Reinvesting Your One and Only Life* (2001). Drucker is also extensively featured in Buford's 2004 book, *Finishing Well: What People Who Really Live Do Differently!*

Buford moved from being a successful cable television executive in Texas into a Drucker-like multipronged career. Although he is now in his late sixties, he has hardly slowed down. In addition to his work as an author, he also leads the Leadership Network, which helps to connect and provide information sources for innovative churches. For Buford, a strong Christian faith has been an integral part of his reinvention, and has helped him to deal with the death of Ross, his only son, who drowned in 1987 at the age of twenty-four. Buford movingly relates this story in *Halftime*.

As Drucker noted in the foreword to *Stuck in Halftime*

and elsewhere, today's knowledge workers have a challenging dichotomy: we have unprecedented options for living a long, meaningful, and productive life, yet most of us are unprepared for the challenge. We possibly have so many options that we become confused and frozen in what Swarthmore College professor Barry Schwartz calls "the paradox of choice."

Drucker recommends the self-management of introspection to determine who you are and what you are good at, which we discussed in Chapter 1. This directly relates to the core competencies message of Chapter 2. Buford has noted that we are more prepared for the first half of life, when we have a steady progression from one type of schooling to another, followed by careers. We can take advantage of career guidance and other kinds of guidance offered to students.

But this type of structured help has not been offered to people focusing on how to plan for and live in the second half of their lives. If anything, most of the advice tends to be about finances. As important as that is, it leaves out important, managed decisions about alternatives like different forms of work and generosity. Drucker has said that the leaders and role models for the rest of so-

ASK YOURSELF

If I were to design the perfect university class (open to anyone over twenty-two) on creating a satisfying second half of life, what would I like to learn from it? If I had my choice of anyone in the world to speak to my class, who are some of the people I would choose, and what specifically would I hope to learn from them?

Drucker was the perfect advertisement for living a meaningful second half of life. He demonstrated that you don't necessarily have to change the things you do after the age of forty. He continued with his combined careers of writing, teaching, and consulting. The majority of his books were written after he turned sixty-five. But as he got older, he made adjustments. He decreased his teaching load, and only took on consulting clients who would travel to his home in Claremont, California.

ciety will be people who successfully manage the second half of life. As of now, most of us are on our own, and it's up to us to plan for and navigate this crucial transition.

Second Careers

We will have to learn to develop second careers for accomplished professional and managerial people when they reach their late forties or so.[50]

IN DRUCKER'S ESTIMATION, a knowledge worker continually needs fresh challenges and new stimulation to keep growing in work and life. The world changes rapidly, and it's all too easy to become irrelevant. One deceptively simple idea that he long advocated was the development of a second career, which doesn't necessarily have to be a radical shift from your present job. If you love a particular kind of work, but are tired of the setting in which you perform that activity, it may be time to consider shifting the setting. "Often this means," Drucker wrote, "only moving from one kind of organization to another."[51] This doesn't necessarily mean doing exactly the same kind of work for a different company. That would just be a change of jobs and setting, which might be valuable on its own, but wouldn't qualify as a second career. Examples of what Drucker meant might be a lawyer moving from a law firm into running the legal department of a nonprofit for a cause he or she really believes in; a doctor leaving an established practice to start a medical clinic for low-income people; a newspaper or magazine photographer moving into photographing weddings and related family events.

This is the type of shift—of both work and mindset—that Buford calls "success to significance." It is not a matter of someone who has not yet found success in life looking for something different. It is someone who has found success leveraging that success in a new way, with new meaning, and for new people. It is a success that is important to you personally, that resonates with your values, and is not necessarily meant to be what other people deem successful. Drucker also saw it as the search for a new community. How do you get the most meaning out of your current work? What would you have to change? What first step can you take today?

Drucker pointed out—and this will be discussed further in Chapter 5—that the second career (and the second half of life in general) may require more schooling. He noted the increasing number of middle-aged people—particularly women—entering law school. He also saw a similar phenomenon in the age of people entering theological seminaries.

When considering a second career, it's helpful to consider these two aspects: do you want to do something that is an extension of what you are already doing, or do you want something different that emphasizes different parts of who you are? A second career can finally provide the opportunity to do what you've always wanted to do, but, because of circumstances in your life, were not able to do until now.

Drucker noted the phenomenon in America of people who take early retirement but keep on working in a different job, for a different employer or employers. This of course has become much more pronounced with the aging of the baby boomers. Many people are sufficiently financially secure that they can do this without too much trouble. But for many others, early retirement is either not an option or too great a financial stretch. As the economy ebbs and flows, some people who planned to retire early miscalculated, as the cost of living—particularly health care and energy—rises dramatically. Then either they are completely forced out of retirement, or they want to work part time, if not exactly at a new career.

Second careers need not be traumatic shifts, although this career shift does take thought and consideration. The ability to think like a CEO (described in Chapter 1) is needed for this kind of decision. If you think like a CEO when considering a second career, you consider the effect such a move will have not only on you, but on your family and other associates, your current workplace, the community, and even society in general. What steps can you start taking today to plan for a second career? What impact might they have on the work you do now?

In an interview with author/journalist Harriet Rubin, Drucker said, "Most of us, if we live long enough, must change careers. If career planning means not being open to opportunity, it doesn't work. Planning should tell you only which opportunities are the right ones for you and which are the wrong ones."[52] This quote comes from "Peter's Principles," Rubin's *Inc.* magazine article of March 1998, an insightful and entertaining look at how Drucker advised her when she left her job running a business publishing company to work on her own as an author and adviser. It is still available on the Web and is well worth reading for the advice Drucker gave during Rubin's daylong pilgrimage to his house in Claremont.

Finally, Drucker delighted in being provocative, giving his readers something to think about and really digest. Consider this interview response he gave, thirty years earlier, in 1968 for *Psychology Today.* "The older professions," he said, "are best suited to become second careers. Middle age is really the best time to switch to being the lawyer, the teacher, the priest, the doctor—I shocked you—and the social worker."[53]

ASK YOURSELF

How would my choice of a second career differ from my first? Would I be looking primarily for work with more meaning and significance, and, if so, would income or a lack of it matter to me?

How fascinating to think that he gave this answer back in the days when the first baby boomers were just finishing college. Baby boomers who would have been in high school, college, or who were recent college graduates at that time may now, at middle age and even near traditional retirement age, be faced with a second career decision. Teaching and the clergy have become popular choices for this shift, but Drucker may have been too far ahead of his time regarding changes in the medical profession.

Drucker's second career came in his late twenties and early thirties, when he moved from working in banking and finance to writing, first as a journalist and soon after as an author. This involved a shift from his comfort zone, but he was much better suited to writing than working in the financial world. Consider what millions of eventual readers would have missed had Drucker never made the move! He later added his other parallel careers of teaching and consulting. This mix of three interrelated careers continued for the rest of his life.

Parallel Careers

The second answer to the question of what to do with the second half of one's life is to develop a parallel career.[54]

DRUCKER WROTE THIS PASSAGE in his 1999 book *Management Challenges for the 21st Century*. He gave three answers to navigate a successful second half of life. The first was to develop a second career, the second was to have a parallel career, and the third answer was social entrepreneurship, which will be discussed in Chapter 4. Just like second careers, the world of parallel careers is full of options. The parallel career can be quite beneficial, providing both psychic and financial rewards for knowledge workers who put in the time, effort, and thought to work simultaneously on two (or more) jobs. It's much more of a commitment than merely having a part-time job, though technically it could fall into that category.

Drucker uses the word "create," which is a good way to approach discussing parallel careers. A parallel career is something that didn't previously exist in your life, and you must be creative in your approach to make it happen. He also was careful to note that a parallel career had to be noncompetitive with your main career. If, for example, you are a business executive, it would be acceptable to become a consultant to nonprofit organizations, but not to become an entrepreneur in direct competition with your own company.

Parallel careers can eventually morph into your main career, or become your second or post-retirement career. Just as Drucker was a big proponent of pilot testing of products and services in the business world, he also advocated that people pilot test their parallel or second career. One of Drucker's own choices of parallel careers—teaching—will be discussed more fully in Chapter 5.

In *Management Challenges for the 21st Century*, Drucker noted other possibilities that he said more commonly occur in nonprofit organizations. The implication here is that some jobs will be paid work, and others will be on a volunteer basis. This will be a decision knowledge workers must make: whether or not money should be a factor in a parallel career. Drucker cites some examples of nonprofit parallel careers: running shelters, working in a local public library, participating in the administration of your church, or becoming the president of your local Girl Scouts council.

A major reason for carving out a parallel career is also valid for contributions made as a volunteer or with a serious outside interest: the scope it gives knowledge workers for a different level of success that may not be available in your main job. Drucker wrote that while every knowledge worker aspires to success, this is not always possible. But when we perform more self-directed work of our own choosing, for a cause greater than ourselves as individuals and for the benefit of other people, we have the opportunity to truly be a success, and to see our contributions in action. We can feel like a more important person who makes a difference and has an impact. Drucker said this is vital not only for the knowledge worker, but for his or her family as well.

Some people seek a parallel career because, while they fundamentally enjoy their main job, they need additional stimulation from other types of work. Another potential reason is lack of advancement or promotion opportunities. In 1995, Drucker told interviewer T. George Harris (his longtime friend and sometime collaborator) of the *Harvard Business Review*: "The stepladder is gone, and there's not even the implied structure of an industry's rope ladder. It's more like vines, and you bring your own machete."[55] He made two other profound observations about parallel careers. One is that they give you a window into other worlds. You will work with and for people who think and act differently, and have different concerns. They may open your eyes to new ways of thinking and seeing, and new levels of empathy for others.

ASK YOURSELF

How well do opportunities for a parallel career, perhaps in a nonprofit organization, match my values, experience, and education? What shifts would I have to make in my life to make these changes?

The second observation is that a parallel career—especially one that involves working in a nonprofit, as we'll see in Chapter 4—may provide leadership opportunities that are not available in your main job. These are valuable in their own right and can give you leadership experience

Drucker managed to juggle his parallel careers of writing, teaching, and consulting. Each was important to him, and had its own demands of time and attention. One of the reasons he was able to make it work was that each was nourished by the others. The experience he gained from working in each career, and the benefits of the knowledge and friendship he gained from the people in each, became elements employed in the other disciplines. His experiences in consulting were particularly important to his books and articles, and in the classroom.

that can be put to use in the future in your main job. One of Drucker's gifts is that he makes the challenge of being a better person—not just a better knowledge worker—seem sensible, reasonable, imperative, and doable. He never said it would be easy. He also knew that the world would be a better place if we all had fulfilling work, in whatever category, that made a difference to society.

Portable and Mobile

The means of production is knowledge, which is owned by knowledge workers and is highly portable.[56]

THE CONCEPTS OF PORTABILITY and mobility provide the foundation for the options we have in creating second or parallel careers, and are crucial in our main careers as well. We are less tied to one particular job, industry, or geographical location than workers of previous generations. If we use our core competencies and continue to develop them, we can more easily move from one employer to another, in the same line of work or otherwise. Our skills are portable, and so is our technology. We now use smaller and smaller hardware to access large amounts of increasingly sophisticated software. We no longer have to carry around masses of paper because we can access most of our files from anywhere on the Web. This is a major advantage over the options available to the readers of Drucker's earlier books, the knowledge workers of a less technological age.

Knowledge workers can accept work from people they may never actually see, who live thousands of miles away. Advances in telecommunications and computing have made this possible, and these advances will only become more sophisticated and elaborate in the future. A worker's knowledge and ability to learn provide the raw material for work that can span boundaries. If our knowledge is portable, we can work from anywhere. We are not necessarily tied to one line of work, especially as new types of jobs are created. Think of how many jobs related to the Web and to mobile phones didn't even exist as recently as the late 1980s. In a knowledge society, everything revolves around how knowledge is used. The products and services we buy and use are the result of people putting knowledge to work. Everything starts off as an idea, or as a creative combination of ideas.

Mass communications enhance our ability to work for a company on the other side of the globe, while the vastly improved worldwide transportation system, launched in the mid-twentieth century, enables us to move anywhere in the world and not be tied to one geographical area as our forebears may have been.

However, although we are portable and mobile, Drucker emphasized that most knowledge workers still need access to an organization to bring their work to fruition. He also pointed out that individuals needed the complementary talents of others to bring their work to light. He believed that there were few "lone geniuses."

Stop to consider how the work you do is affected or fully realized by an organization of one type or another. There are probably very few knowledge workers who can say they work totally on their own, without involving an organization of some type somewhere in the process. This awareness may serve you well as you consider your options for second or parallel careers.

Mobility and portability grant us freedom and can help us carry out our lives not only in parallel and second careers, but also in the activities to be discussed in the next chapter, such as volunteerism or mentorship. Mobility and portability are also crucial to the multidimensional activities we'll discuss in Chapter 5, "Teaching and Learning."

ASK YOURSELF

How portable are my skills in my current job? Do they lend themselves to being applied in different industries or even in different countries?

Because of improved technology, knowledge workers can teach for schools anywhere in the world, working with students they may never meet in person. They can use mobile and portable technology to learn through similar online classes, or just from what is available on the Web.

These possibilities didn't exist when Drucker wrote many of his most important books, particularly *The Effective Executive* in 1967. But now mobility and portability must factor in to all of our decisions about leading a multidimensional life. They also bring us the relatively new danger of being tethered to the job 24/7. Although this was possible before the days

Drucker's mobility decreased as he became older, but he didn't necessarily need to be mobile to write books and articles, to teach at Claremont, or to consult with clients who were willing to travel to his home. He also provides a case in point that no matter how capable knowledge workers are, they still need access to an organization to realize their talents. In his own case, as brilliant and influential as he was, he still needed a university at which to teach, publishers to bring his writing to the public, and companies and other organizations to consult for that served as sources and "laboratories" for his ideas.

of instant, high-speed access to the Web and sophisticated mobile phones, these technologies make it easier for employers to expect knowledge workers to be available at all hours. Whether this is enhanced or diminished by engaging in multidimensional activities is a decision each knowledge worker must consider based on the individual's situation.

Reinvention

> People change over such a long time span. They become different persons with different needs, different abilities, different perspectives and therefore, with a need to "reinvent themselves."[57]

DRUCKER WROTE THIS PASSAGE in "Reinventing the Individual," a chapter in *Drucker on Asia*, a series of written dialogues between Drucker and the late Japanese retailing magnate Isao Nakauchi. The chapter is one of four separate chapters on reinvention, along with one each on business, society, and government. Drucker makes an intriguing point about the need for reinvention. The person you are reinventing is no longer who you were when you were younger. It sounds obvious, but makes the most sense only in retrospect and with reflection. We must reinvent ourselves for our new circumstances. What we learned in school and through experience has brought us to a certain point, but now it's time for new learning and experiences.

In *Drucker on Asia*, Drucker noted that today's climate calls for change beyond the ordinary. "You have to make something different out of yourself," Drucker writes, "rather than just find a new supply of energy."[58] His prescriptions are given through his own life experience, especially his early years of work and learning. Reinvention usually means going outside of your comfort zone. It can mean making a new professional life based on new skills, new knowledge, and new people. It may mean using your mobility to move to a new locality, or using your portability to work remotely for an employer based far away from your home.

Drucker on Asia was first published in Japan in 1995, just as the World Wide Web was making its first, tentative impact. It would be three years before Google arrived. People have more scope for reinvention now, and more ways to accomplish and to learn how to do it. There are many informative books to give us examples of people who made successful reinventions at different stages of life, such as Mark Albion's *Making a Life, Making a Living* and Po Bronson's *What Should I Do With My Life?*

An outstanding example of reinvention is Doris Drucker, who accomplished two reinventions in her life after the age of eighty. She was born in Germany and studied throughout Europe before marrying Peter. After they immigrated to the United States in 1937, she worked in a variety of jobs, including editor and registered patent agent. In 1963, she earned a physics degree from Fairleigh Dickinson University in New Jersey. In her mid-eighties, she invented a voice monitor called a Visivox, which is used by speech therapists and in auditoriums for monitoring the sound level of speakers. Rather than license her invention to another company, she and a partner formed a company, RSQ, to market the invention. After she turned ninety, her memoirs, *Invent Radium or I'll Pull Your Hair*, were published by the University of Chicago Press in 2004. It's a wonderful book, mainly about her life leading up to coming to the United States with her husband in 1937. It shows her to be a powerful writer and storyteller. Her life example demonstrates that it's never too late for personal change and reinvention.

Although reinvention can be highly valid for the second half of one's life, it need not happen only at that stage. Leaving college or graduate school to enter the workforce can provide an opportunity to accomplish this type of change. So can almost any event at any age along our career paths. Sometimes it's not necessary, but sometimes your hand is forced. Your organization may have been

ASK YOURSELF

What specifically do I admire about people who have reinvented their lives? What can I learn from their experience that would give me ideas for my own possible reinvention?

Drucker had to reinvent himself when he came to the United States in 1937. Even though he was doing work similar to what he did in Europe (journalism), he had to perform it in a new country. Though he continued writing as a correspondent for British newspapers, he had to find new outlets for his journalism. Two years after he arrived, he further reinvented himself as an author, with his first book, *The End of Economic Man*. In some ways, he continued to reinvent himself until his death, as he found ways to remain relevant to his readers, students, and clients long after many of his contemporaries were retired or dead.

closed, or sold, or downsized. You may have to move to a new location. You may become bored with your job and no longer find fulfillment or excitement in it.

Reinvention is bolder and more exciting than merely finding a new job, or deciding what one is going to do upon turning forty-five or sixty-five. It requires deep thought, creativity, the desire and ability to change, and the willingness to reach out to others.

Chapter Question Summaries

The Second Half of Your Life   Think about what an ideal university course (open to anyone over twenty-two) would entail for preparing you for the second half of life.

Second Careers   Think about what you'd want out of a second career, especially if you seek meaning more than money.

Parallel Careers Think about the match you need between your values and opportunities for a parallel career.

Portable and Mobile Think about how portable your skills really are, and if they lend themselves to working in other industries, or even other countries.

Reinvention Think about people you know who have reinvented themselves, and if they can be possible role models for you.

Chapter Recap and Next Steps

In this chapter we investigated how you can create your future by thinking about second and parallel careers, and by reinventing yourself. We have covered:

» Drucker's emphasis on the importance of planning for the second half of your life
» The strategic thinking that goes into considering a second career
» The wisdom of creating a parallel career that may one day become your main career
» The portability and mobility of our knowledge, and how technology makes it easier for us to apply that knowledge beyond geographic borders
» How Drucker identified the need for personal reinvention as early as 1995, and how reinventing ourselves means leaving our comfort zone for new people, new work, and new challenges

In Chapter 4, some of these items will connect with the expression of generosity involved in such areas as volunteerism, mentorship, and social entrepreneurship.

Hints for Creating Your Total Life List

If you are on Facebook, LinkedIn, or similar social networking sites, read as many profiles as you can of people on your list of friends or associates. Examine their career journeys, including the types of career experience they've had, as well as their educational experience.

See what patterns and commonalities there are among people, especially those who appear to have more than one or parallel careers, or who have reinvented themselves. What can you learn from these people? Could you contact them to benefit from their wisdom? Is there any help you can offer them in return?

If you are not on these sites, ask people you admire about how their careers unfolded. Find out if they have had second or parallel careers, or have reinvented themselves, or if this is something they are planning for the future. Again, look for ways you can offer to help them in return.

Besides looking at these sites for ideas on career journeys, you can expand your search to try to get more of a sense of the Total Life of each person. Pay particular attention to those who display a solid mix of work and outside activities. Contact them and find out if they will discuss how they manage their time to get the most out of all these activities and their interactions with others. If possible, meet them for discussion in person, as well as contacting them online.

It also pays to regularly scan each person's list of friends to give you ideas for people you'd like to add not only to your own list of online friends, but also as valuable additions to your "offline" life.

The same concept applies if you are not on these sites. Identify the people you know who seem to be able to fit in fulfilling work and nonwork activities. Find out more about how they accomplish it, and how you can help them in return. Could any people or activities in their life become part of yours?

FOUR

Exercising Your Generosity

We are creating tomorrow's society of citizens through the non-profit service institution. And in that society, everybody is a leader, everybody is responsible, everybody acts.[59]

As you create and modify your Total Life List, one of the most crucial aspects of living a life of more than one dimension is how you display your sense of generosity. Sharing your time and talents in areas such as non-profit work and volunteerism, social entrepreneurship, mentoring, and servant leadership provides opportunities to deepen your work and personal experience, while widening your circle of friends and associates. All these areas involve generosity with your knowledge, your contacts, and possibly even your money. They can be valuable complements to other work you do and can significantly enrich your sense of meaning.

Drucker was extremely generous with his time. He had an almost unlimited number of offers for lecturing, consulting, writing, presenting, and so on. He could have worked much more on these lucrative activities, yet he spent considerable time helping his former students—such as in helping them find jobs—and doing pro bono work for nonprofits. He also mentored a number of people. This spirit of generosity adds to Drucker's reputation as a role model. It also reflects what we learned in Chapter 2 about focusing on achievement rather than making money.

However, there are potential challenges and downsides to exercising the spirit of generosity. One is the time commitment, which could be more than you are willing and able to give, especially if you have more than one volunteer or nonprofit activity. Some volunteer work can be very intense, physically, mentally, and emotionally, and you could develop burnout similar to what you might experience in your main job. You might also be frustrated by the people you try to help, who might not always be capable of helping themselves or letting you help them.

But Drucker's key idea here is that the really important things happen outside your workplace, in other industries, professions, and walks of life. One way to find out about these areas is to volunteer or work with other organizations in different areas from your own. You'll interact with people who have diverse life experiences and bring different strengths from your own. You'll see parts of society that you don't experience in your daily employment. All this contributes to your self-development and the ability to learn new things.

Volunteerism

They are knowledge workers in the jobs in which they earn their living, and they want to be knowledge workers in the jobs in which they contribute to society—that is, their volunteer work. [60]

DRUCKER SAW VOLUNTEERISM AS essential to the smooth functioning of society. Although he had worked with government institutions, he felt that government could not solve all of society's problems, and that nonprofit agencies, with a backbone of strong, committed volunteers, were a valid way of tackling this work.

There are many volunteering opportunities within nonprofits that can provide meaningful work outside of the traditional workplace, because there is no end to the problems and challenges faced by society and our fellow citizens. We can go out and make ourselves useful, as Drucker advised *Good to Great* author Jim Collins to do years ago. This is an avenue where knowledge workers can shine and blossom. You can have an importance, an elevated role that may not be possible in your main job or profession.

A few of the hundreds of options for volunteering include devoting a certain amount of time each week or month to:

» Homeless shelters
» Animal shelters or animal rescue organizations
» Religious institutions
» Libraries, reading programs, and literacy tutoring programs

» Professional organizations or charities (including serving on boards of directors)

Some of the knowledge workers who were interviewed for this book also gave of their time and talents to such areas as working with a local chamber of commerce, volunteering in hospitals and hospices, in museums and other cultural institutions, being Girl Scout leaders, and volunteering in schools.

There may be times when our jobs no longer challenge us, or do not challenge us in the right way. We need to stretch. Many of us can look out at the horizon of our present career and see many benefits, but we may or may not see new challenges. We may hunger for the chance to lead people, but see no prospect for it in our present job. Satisfying this hunger and pursuing and meeting these challenges are still possible in a parallel career in a nonprofit, social-sector organization. For instance, while working in a nonprofit organization, you may discover hidden skills or learn new ones. Or you may be asked to take on a task that you never would have in your regular work. You may find you have an aptitude for it, and run with it.

In a 2002 speech to librarians in Los Angeles, Drucker outlined a simple formula for finding a good volunteer opportunity: Find an organization that fits your values, something you believe in, and work for it. He also emphasized that in your role as a volunteer, you meet different types of people. Volunteerism also ensures that your main job doesn't consume your life.

The volunteerism expert and longtime nonprofit and business executive John Raynolds has noted "the halo effect" of volunteering in his 1998 book of the same name. He contends that beyond the valuable work you do as a volunteer, employers tend to think better of you for your contributions. A successful volunteering experience, to put it bluntly, looks good on your résumé. Many companies have in-house volunteering programs, in which employees get involved in a wide range of areas, such as literacy tutoring or building homes for Habitat for Humanity.

The Web provides many sources for finding volunteerism opportunities in your community. One of the best sites is VolunteerMatch, at www.volunteermatch.org, in which you can type in your zip code and your interests and find out about specific organizations that can use your talents, or help you develop new ones. Similarly, nonprofits can also advertise their needs on the site. The Points of Light Institute is another source of these opportunities, as is your local public library. You may also gain more insights from the Web sites of your local community volunteer agencies, the United Way, or similar organizations. Another Web outlet is Craigslist: visit www.craigslist.org, find your city or area, and click on the volunteer link in the community section, which will automatically lead you to volunteerism opportunities in your local area.

Also consider: Do you prefer to volunteer by performing knowledge work—such as marketing, financial, or legal tasks—or physical work? Some people may want a break from knowledge work and would prefer physical work, for example, by helping at a soup kitchen or building homes for Habitat for Humanity. Training is often available in these situations so you don't necessarily need prior experience. This is an ironic twist on Drucker's differentiation between manual and knowledge workers. In this case, manual work can be equally as fulfilling as what you do with your mind.

The idea of national service is now slowly but steadily taking hold, especially for young people. It is the focus of *America the Principled*, the 2007 book by Harvard Business School professor Rosabeth Moss Kanter. In 2007, *Time* magazine had a major cover feature, "A Time to Serve," on the benefit of service to society. National service would provide younger and older people a structured opportunity to develop their skills, contribute work to nonprofits, and gain some benefits such as scholarship funds.

Such a program would go beyond personal gains to strengthening the entire nonprofit sector of the United States, and thereby improving the quality of life for everyone in the country. As examples, the *Time* article cites City Year (which includes Kanter among its board of trustees) and other social entrepreneurship ventures, such as Teach for America, started in 1989 by Wendy Kopp, which sends recent college graduates to teach for a year in challenging inner-city schools.

"A Time to Serve" outlines a ten-point plan, which includes making national service a cabinet-level department, and greatly expanding relatively small but success-

ASK YOURSELF

Do I have friends or colleagues who currently volunteer? Could I talk to some of them about the pros and cons of their experience? Does my volunteer work have to tie in with a sense of meaning, or am I looking more for new challenges or new people?

Drucker did a significant amount of pro bono consulting for nonprofit organizations, including the Girl Scouts of the USA, the Salvation Army, religious institutions, and the American Red Cross. He received the Evangeline Booth Award, its highest honor, from the Salvation Army in 2001. A book published in the same year, *"The Most Effective Organization in the U.S.": Leadership Secrets of the Salvation Army*, by army commissioner Robert A. Watson and Ben Brown, takes its title from a quote by Drucker. This book also contains considerable material about Drucker and his views on the importance of nonprofit organizations and volunteerism.

ful current programs such as AmeriCorps. An intriguing element of the plan is the proposal to create a national service academy, a kind of nonmilitary West Point.

In 2005 the disaster of Hurricane Katrina elicited myriad types of service and volunteerism. Many people found life-changing opportunities helping people and communities rebuild their lives. In some cases, they combined this with their faith and spiritual values by joining with others in their religious communities to stay for extended periods of time in New Orleans and other affected areas.

Nonprofit Organizations

The first lesson business executives can learn from successful nonprofits is to begin with mission.[61]

IN 1990, THREE OF Drucker's longtime associates—Frances Hesselbein, Bob Buford, and Richard F. Schubert—formed the Peter F. Drucker Foundation for Nonprofit Management (now the Leader to Leader Institute). Hesselbein had recently retired as CEO of the Girl Scouts of the USA and she became the chairman of the new organization. We met Buford, the former cable television entrepreneur turned author/social entrepreneur, in Chapter 3. Schubert is a former president of the American Red Cross, among other organizations. All had considerable leadership experience and were friendly with Drucker, in addition to having worked closely with him in consulting relationships in the past.

Drucker remained an active honorary chairman of the organization until 2002, thus underscoring his commitment to nonprofits and the crucial role they play by helping to cure society's ills, and by providing meaningful work and leadership opportunities for large numbers of people. The Leader to Leader Institute remains committed to strengthening the leadership of the nonprofit sector and publishes a journal, *Leader to Leader*, which has included material by and about Drucker. Some of these pieces have been collected in book anthologies.

One of Drucker's most important books is *Managing the Non-Profit Organization: Practices and Principles*, published the same year as the launch of the Drucker Foun-

Drucker's longtime work with nonprofit organizations was particularly important in the bridge he helped build between them and the for-profit sector. He was able to help these organizations through his pro bono consulting and his work with the Drucker Foundation. Although his title was that of honorary chairman, he was quite active and involved in its growth and influence. But he also sought to convince the business world that the nonprofit sector should be seen as an opportunity for learning and partnership and should be taken seriously.

dation. Much of the book consists of interviews Drucker conducted with nonprofit leaders, including Buford and Hesselbein. He also spoke with business leaders such as Max De Pree, who was chairman and CEO of the innovative furniture design company Herman Miller at the time, and a member of the board of the Fuller Theological Seminary. But there is also eloquently written material from Drucker's own life.

Drucker wrote about an angle of nonprofits that few had considered in "What Business Can Learn from Nonprofits," an article for the July–August 1989 *Harvard Business Review* (later collected in the book *Classic Drucker*). He knew businesses could profit from the example of organizations that had to make contributions meaningful for a volunteer work force. He advocated that businesses would ultimately have to treat their own knowledge workers in a similar fashion, because the workers' mobility meant they could leave at any time.

A related area of nonprofits is important to consider,

and that is financial support. Many knowledge workers make financial contributions on a regular basis to non-profit agencies of all types, religious and secular. Some who are particularly well off financially enjoy being bene-factors. One possible activity in the second half of life is managing one's personal philanthropy, especially if large sums of money or family foundations are involved.

One way knowledge workers can get involved with a nonprofit is to consider joining—or possibly starting—a Drucker Society. These organizations will give you regu-lar contact with people who may have interests and values similar to your own. If you're interested in what role you can play in a strong community and society, with organi-zations of capable, ethical leaders, it's worth investigating. The most robust societies are currently in Asia, but more are developing rapidly in the United States, Canada, Eu-rope, and South America. The societies operate under the umbrella of the Drucker Institute (of which Bob Buford is the chairman), the Claremont-based organization that seeks to further Drucker's ideas for the good of society worldwide.

You can learn more about the institute and these soci-eties, their important work, and how you can participate, at the Drucker Institute's Web site, www.druckerinstitute .com. At the same site you'll find information about Drucker from the digitized collections of the Drucker Ar-chives. You can access a wealth of his material, including personal letters written to him by many different people, free of charge. These give an insight into Drucker's impact on individuals and organizations. Seeing what he did for others can give you ideas for how you'd like to make a similar impact for people.

Rick Wartzman on The Drucker Institute and The Drucker Societies

I asked Rick Wartzman, the director of the Drucker Institute in Claremont, California, to describe the Drucker Societies in more depth and to give an idea of how people could get involved.

1. What are some practical ways knowledge workers can get involved in one of the Drucker Societies? Do they have to live in a particular geographical area to become a member, and are there certain qualifications for membership?

Drucker Societies are all-volunteer groups that draw on Peter Drucker's ideas and ideals about effective management and ethical leadership to bring about positive change in their local communities. The Drucker Society Global Network is young, having been formed only in 2007. But by late 2008, under the guidance of the Drucker Institute at Claremont Graduate University, the Societies were beginning to implement a series of programs that are decidedly Druckeresque in their focus: centered on community and geared toward action and achieving measurable results.

As of late 2008, there were about a dozen Drucker Societies in operation around the world, and different Societies were applying Drucker's insights in different ways. In Dallas and in Brazil, for instance, Society volunteers were taking steps to train nonprofit and nongovernmental organization (NGO) leaders in various Drucker management principles through a half-day workshop developed by the Drucker Institute. In South Korea, senior corporate executives were gathering regularly to read Drucker's work and to figure out how to put his teachings into practice in their companies and, increasingly, in their communities. In Los Angeles and New York and the Philippines, Drucker Society volunteers were preparing to roll out a program to teach basic management concepts to eleventh- and twelfth-graders—and then have the students put those ideas into action by designing and completing their own community-service projects.

If you're interested in getting involved in a Drucker Society, you can join an existing one near you. Just check the Drucker Institute Web site (www.druckerinstitute .com) to see if there is a society in your area. If there is none, you can apply to start your own Drucker Society. Applications and additional information are available on the Institute's Web site, as well. (Just click on the button on the homepage that says "Creating Global Change.")

2. Are there particular ways that people who want to live and work in the Drucker spirit can get involved in the Drucker Institute?

The Drucker Society Global Network is the best way for those who want to live and work in the Drucker spirit to get involved; the Drucker Societies are where ideas get turned into action. The Drucker Institute, for its part, serves as the hub of the network, supporting the activities of existing Societies and seeding new Societies.

3. How do you recommend that readers get the most benefit out of the work of the Drucker Institute and/or Society, whether or not they are members?

The best way to reap the benefit of a Drucker Society is, of course, to join one.

If you can't make that kind of volunteer time commitment, however, you may want to invite a nearby Drucker Society to visit your company, nonprofit group, or government agency to make a presentation of some kind. Every Drucker Society, for example, is eligible to deliver the Drucker Institute's signature communications tool— a presentation called "Closing the Responsibility Gap." This 45-minute show explains how, as a society, we've not been very good stewards of our institutions, our people, our resources, or our values—and suggests some ways, based on Drucker's insights, to make things better.

You can also contact the Drucker Institute directly to arrange to have the "Responsibility Gap" presented to your organization.

What Is the Drucker Society of New York City?

BY LEE IGEL

I asked Lee Igel, a management professor at New York University who leads the Peter Drucker Society of New York City, to write a brief description of its activities:

The mission of the Peter Drucker Society of New York City is: to convert the Drucker principles into action across the community. Members of the Society act on the mission primarily through monthly meetings. These meetings generally consist of discussion built upon newsworthy events or topics of hot debate, and are supported by relevant readings from the enormous amount of thought left to us by Peter Drucker. Once in a while, depending on the theme of the meeting, we will supplement the Drucker work with that of colleagues, thinkers, clients, and friends whom Peter Drucker personally inspired at some point in time.

In any case, the objective of the meetings is not for members to participate in an evening of intellectual conversation, the style of which might have been seen in a European salon of the nineteenth century. Rather, the objective is for each member to think through real issues of human affairs, to listen to and gather insight from other members, to understand how the Drucker principles can be applied, and to take action with what has been learned. Yes, we attempt to find the other side of the question "What would Peter Drucker have said?" But we really concentrate far more on asking and finding answers to the question "What needs to be done?"

Let me also say that the membership of the Drucker Society of New York City purposefully and proudly reflects the city itself. The society is composed of people from a constellation of professional and personal backgrounds. And so we welcome the idea that some members variously choose or find that they have time to come only to monthly meetings, while others add to that by working on projects generated within the Society and in partnership with other Drucker Societies and the Drucker Institute. The thinking here is that people lead busy lives and are heavily involved in all manner of things, especially given that this all happens in "the city that never sleeps." But there is an enormous capacity for doing and for the results that come from it. That is, members of the Drucker Society recognize that management gives us what is needed to perform in ways that benefit those around us. It is how we believe we could more thoughtfully and effectively contribute to our community.

Social Entrepreneurship

> And then, finally, the third answer—there are the "social entrepreneurs." These are usually people who have been very successful in their first profession, as businessmen, as physicians.... They love their work, but it no longer challenges them.... [T]hey start another, and usually a non-profit, activity.[62]

THIS PASSAGE FROM DRUCKER'S 1999 book *Management Challenges for the 21st Century* comes from his three answers to navigating a successful second half of life (see Chapter 3). As interest in entrepreneurship and innovation has grown—especially since Drucker's 1985 landmark book *Innovation and Entrepreneurship*—many people are pairing those concepts with an interest in making a profound difference in the world. Social entrepreneurs—people who use organizational thinking and entrepreneurship to effect social change—either zero in on causes that haven't been well served by existing nonprofits, or approach them in a different way. You can become one at almost any stage of life, not necessarily the second half.

Social entrepreneurship is an area that is hot and even hip now, but Drucker wrote about it years before it achieved this status. These special entrepreneurs combine passion with a fierce commitment to their cause. If they didn't have both qualities, their organizations would not last long. Doing this kind of work takes time, requires money and continual fund-raising, and the ability to get other people to believe in your cause and in your ability to do something productive about it. Sometimes this comes in the form of public-private partnerships with corporations, or in creating for-profit ventures to raise money.

As you read about the social entrepreneurs and their organizations in this chapter, think about how their stories might apply to your own personal situation. Is this something you might aspire to in the future, either in becoming a social entrepreneur, or in working or volunteering for one? Is there anything in their backgrounds that are similar to yours? Are you prepared for the commitment of time and possibly money that social entrepreneurship often entails? Building a new nonprofit organization takes tremendous personal fortitude, and a thick skin for rejection.

ASK YOURSELF

Do I see areas where my role as a social entrepreneur might be changed or strengthened by partnering with other, similar organizations to avoid overlap? Do I think I personally can best address societal ills as a social entrepreneur, working with an established nonprofit, or partnering with a well-meaning for-profit business?

An especially good book that gets inside the mind of a successful social entrepreneur—and that can help you gauge whether you can marshal the right levels of passion and commitment—is Bill Shore's *The Cathedral Within* (1999). It describes his work for his own anti-hunger nonprofit, Share Our Strength, and the work of other social entrepreneurs. Another is David Bornstein's 2004 book *How to Change the World: Social Entrepreneurs and the Power of New Ideas*, which surveys the world of social entrepreneurship with case studies of people and organizations that have had impact in local areas and worldwide. Bornstein's earlier book, *The Price of a Dream* (1996), was about the social entrepreneur Mohammad Yunus and his Grameen Bank of Bangladesh; Yunus won the 2006 Nobel Peace Prize for pioneering the concept of micro-lending.

Shore and others have written about City Year, an innovative social entrepreneurship organization begun in 1988 by Harvard students Michael Brown and Alan Khazei that was the prototype for AmeriCorps. It sends young people into the inner city for a year of teaching and mentoring, and has been successful in making valuable use of partnerships with the business world. This program now has a Drucker connection. Ira Jackson, who became dean of the Drucker-Ito School in 2006, has been a longtime supporter of City Year, going back to his days as a Boston banking executive. And in 2008, Allison Graff-Weisner, the executive director of City Year in Los Angeles, was named to the board of advisors of the Drucker Institute.

John Wood detailed his venture into social entrepreneurship in his 2006 book *Leaving Microsoft to Change the World*. He left a high-paying job as a Microsoft executive in Beijing, cashed out his stock options, and started Room to Read, a nonprofit that builds schools and libraries in the developing world, originally in Asian countries and now in Africa as well. Another nonprofit, albeit on a smaller scale, that has begun to develop libraries in Africa is the Lubuto Library Project, started by a Washington, D.C.–based librarian–turned–social entrepreneur, Jane Kinney Meyers. This project aims to build many libraries for street children and other vulnerable children across Africa. The first one opened in September 2007 in Lusaka, Zambia. This venture is an example of an organization that provides meaningful volunteerism opportunities for like-minded people. Meyers has reached out to fellow librarians through areas of contact such as schools of library and information science and the Web site of the social science division of the Special Libraries Association to find people who want to get involved in her project.

Bill Gates is an example of a highly successful business entrepreneur turned social entrepreneur. After cofounding and leading Microsoft, he launched the Bill and Melinda Gates Foundation, which is usefully tackling many serious health and other issues worldwide. In true Drucker-like fashion, Gates is also a prime example of someone who starts a parallel career and eventually eases into making it his main activity. In 2008, he gave up his day-to-day duties at Microsoft to work full-time with his foundation.

This spotlights a situation you may face at different

DRUCKER'S LIFE AND WORK

One of Drucker's main boosts to the world of social entrepreneurship was his recommendation of it as an activity in managing yourself and developing opportunities for the second part of life, as he notes in the quote that opens this section. His books and articles about entrepreneurship help give readers the tools to consider and address how or whether to apply entrepreneurship in their lives.

---

points in your life: you've made enough money in the business world and now want to tackle formidable challenges faced by others around your community or the world. At what point do you make the transition to something you deem to have more meaning? If you decide a change is in order, is social entrepreneurship the best vehicle for creating meaning? Perhaps you are better off working within an existing structure of nonprofit organizations. You may also decide to partner with existing social entrepreneurs in ways that are mutually beneficial to you and them.

There are many other ways to learn more about social entrepreneurship, including organizations such as Ashoka, led by William Drayton, and the Skoll Foundation, an educational and networking source, led by former eBay executive Jeffrey Skoll. Drayton is a pioneer of the concept of social entrepreneurship, having formed Ashoka to provide financial and other backing to social entrepreneurs in the early 1980s; his work is described in the books by Bornstein and Shore. There are also Web sites, such as Social Edge, at www.socialedge.org (run by the Skoll Foundation), and university programs at institutions such as Duke University, Columbia University, and elsewhere. Knowledge workers looking to model Drucker values, and to tackle exciting challenges, may welcome social entrepreneurship as a new phase in their lives. But more than any other area discussed in this chapter, it is one you must enter well prepared and be very committed to accomplishing your goal. It is one thing to start a new volunteerism opportunity, find out it isn't working out as you'd like, and move on to something else. It's another matter entirely to raise money for a new organization and find staff and volunteers, only to realize you'd rather be doing something else.

Servant Leadership

Leadership is lifting a person's vision to higher sights, the raising of a person's performance to a higher standard, the building of a personality beyond its normal limitations.[63]

MAX DE PREE, A LONGTIME Drucker client as head of Herman Miller and an interviewee in *Managing the Non-Profit Organization*, writes about the concept of servant leadership in his books *Leadership Is an Art* and *Leadership Jazz*, and in chapters he has contributed to collections on the topic. Servant leadership focuses on providing the resources for your followers so they can make their most significant contributions. It focuses on the personal growth of those being led, and how this contributes to a purpose higher than any one individual. It puts the follower ahead of the leader. It is thus a highly generous form of leadership, and in line with Drucker's belief that leadership is not based on charisma and flash, but hard work, diligence, and responsibility. It is not about imparting energy to followers, but helping them to release it from within themselves.

The concept of servant leadership was first espoused in the 1970s by the late Robert K. Greenleaf, a veteran AT&T human resources executive turned author and leadership guru. Drucker knew Greenleaf personally, and wrote the foreword to a collection of Greenleaf's writing, *On Becoming a Servant Leader*, in 1996. Servant leadership was not a concept that Drucker wrote about otherwise. But it is in keeping with his view that leaders should be humble and put the needs of their organizations ahead of their own.

Richard F. Schubert says the function of the servant leader is "to support people for whom she or he is responsible...support in the sense of what they need to get their job done."[64] He has a particularly interesting vantage point of leadership, since he has worked across all sectors: the head of both the American Red Cross and the Points of Light Foundation, past president of Bethlehem Steel, and a United States deputy secretary of labor.

A servant leader may or may not be paid. Part of the point of this chapter is that people can enhance their multidimensional lives by exercising their spirit of generosity at work or elsewhere. You can exercise servant leadership even as the highly paid CEO of a business, as well as being a nonpaid leader in the nonprofit sector or elsewhere. Seeing to the needs and personal growth of others—whether or not you are paid for doing it—is a powerful expression of a generous spirit. Whether or not they would call themselves servant leaders, a striking number of Drucker's followers (besides De Pree, Hesselbein, Buford, and Schubert) have been leaders in their own right. Other examples include Roxanne Spillett, president and CEO of Boys & Girls Clubs of America, Kathy Cloninger, CEO of the Girl Scouts USA, William Pollard, retired chairman and CEO of ServiceMaster, and John Bachmann, the retired managing partner of the large brokerage company Edward Jones Co.

ASK YOURSELF

Is there anyone in my workplace, or one in which I've worked previously, whom I would consider to be a servant leader? Which of his or her characteristics had the biggest impact on me? If I consider myself to be a leader, does servant leadership match how I carry out my duties?

Drucker was able to do the most good not by being at the head of any one particular organization, but by being a true thought leader whose ideas can help enrich and improve the lives of millions of people worldwide. His effectiveness is validated by his many high-powered followers who became leaders in their own right.

Mentorship

Just as no one learns as much about a subject as the person who is forced to teach it, no one develops as much as the person who is trying to help others to develop themselves.[65]

DRUCKER INTERVIEWED Max De Pree and others in *Managing the Non-Profit Organization* on the importance of mentorship, both providing it and receiving it. Because mentorship is generally not a formal relationship, the guidelines can be tricky. People have to find ways, either formally or informally, to find a mentor. They may need more than one, and may need to change mentors as their careers grow and develop. Another consideration is whether your mentor will come from within your organization, or outside of it. As the person being mentored, you need a great level of trust that the guidance you receive is correct and appropriate.

Mentorship may be broader than just "showing someone the ropes" in an organization. It can include broader career and life advice that may sometimes be at odds with a person's role in an organization, which means that you have to be careful if your mentor works in the same organization as you.

Nevertheless, extending generosity is as important in mentorship as receiving it. Mentorship can occur in any type of organization, and it can be more general in nature. It provides many of the same benefits of self-satisfaction and self-development as teaching, in a somewhat less structured way. As Drucker notes in the quote that begins this section, mentorship gives benefits to the mentor, not just to the person being mentored. De Pree notes that it's not easy to establish these programs formally in organizations, because chemistry has to develop between two people, and that may not happen if they are formally assigned to work with each other.

ASK YOURSELF

Have mentors played a role in my self-development, and have I acknowledged their contributions later in life? What did they contribute? Have I been a mentor to anyone, either formally or informally, and what have I gained from the experience?

Drucker said that within organizations, leaders should look for people who are good at developing others, and praise and recognize their vital contributions. "I think one needs an enormous amount of responsibility," Drucker wrote, "especially as a beginner, but one also does need a mentor."[66] Finally, he noted the importance of a mentor who can guide your development by asking you to consider if your current activities still make sense, and helping you get the most out of your talents and abilities.

Knowledge workers have many opportunities to play this vital role in the lives of other people. They can do it formally within an organization, or through a formal pro-

In *Managing the Non-Profit Organization*, Drucker relates his experiences (as he has done elsewhere) with his first two bosses, who were strict and demanding, yet willing to listen and encourage him when needed. Although this wasn't a formal mentorship process, it shows how in certain cases even one's superior can take on a mentor-like role. Drucker took on mentoring roles for a number of super-achieving people mentioned earlier in this chapter, such as Bob Buford and John Bachmann.

gram in a professional society or other nonprofit. They can do it informally with friends. Another possibility, if you are a teacher, is mentoring former students, as Drucker did regularly on an informal basis.

Chapter Question Summaries

Volunteerism Think about what you can learn from asking friends and colleagues about their volunteerism experiences. Think also about why you want to volunteer in the first place, whether to add meaning in your life, or for new challenges or meeting new people you might not have met otherwise.

Nonprofit Organizations Think about, if you work in a business, what you can learn from well-run nonprofits. Also, consider what partnership opportunities you can identify with these groups.

Social Entrepreneurship   Consider, if you work in a business, what partnership opportunities you could develop with nonprofits.

Servant Leadership   Think about leaders you work with currently or with whom you've worked in the past, and whether or not they would qualify as servant leaders. Consider whether you fit into that category.

Mentorship   Think about mentors who have aided your personal development, and whether or not you have acknowledged their contributions. Think also of your own role as a mentor, either what you've already done, or what you could do in the future.

Chapter Recap and Next Steps

In this chapter, we have seen how you, as a knowledge worker, can exercise your generosity in a number of productive ways by sharing your time and talents. We have covered:

» How volunteerism not only helps society's endless challenges and problems, but provides opportunities for your personal and professional growth and sense of accomplishment

» The importance of nonprofit agencies in today's society, including a look at two directly related to Peter Drucker: the Leader to Leader Institute and the Drucker Institute

» How social entrepreneurship has created new institutions and new opportunities in the nonprofit sector by harnessing the energy and innovation of entrepreneurs who choose a different route from the business world (though they may partner with it)
» The world of servant leadership, in which leaders express their generosity by making sure the needs of their followers are taken care of before their own
» Why mentorship can provide many of the same psychological benefits as teaching, though in a less structured way

In Chapter 5, "Teaching and Learning," we'll look at the many benefits and opportunities for broadening your life by teaching and lifelong, continuous learning. We'll also see how technology has widened these opportunities far beyond what was available during most of Drucker's life.

Hints for Creating Your Total Life List

As you look at the fourteen categories in your Total Life List that you began in Chapter 1, you'll find that opportunities abound for exercising your generosity, beyond the obvious ones of volunteer activities (category 10), nonprofit organizations and social entrepreneurship (category 11), and mentoring (category 12).

Think of ways to involve some of the other categories, and the people within those categories, in these areas of generosity.

For instance, in the first five categories, which include

family members, colleagues, friends, and people in your network, can you think of ways to involve some of these people in your volunteering or other nonprofit activities? Some families volunteer as a group. You could possibly organize or join something group-related at work or within one of your professional groups.

In professional affiliations and associations (category 7), there are numerous opportunities not only for volunteerism, but for gaining leadership experience at the same time.

In teaching (category 9), you may find opportunities as a volunteer, or a possibility for a social entrepreneurship venture. In the spiritual/religious area (a segment of category 13), there are countless opportunities for volunteerism, mentorship, social entrepreneurship, and servant leadership.

It pays to approach your list creatively, and to remember that it is a living document that you will continually consult, add to, and subtract from. This would be a good time to read through parts of Chapter 2 again on the effective use of time, setting priorities, and systematic abandonment, so you can figure out how you can add these important new areas to your life.

FIVE

Teaching and Learning

It is often being said that in the information age every enterprise has to become a learning institution. It also has to become a teaching institution.[67]

The worlds of teaching and learning were intertwined in Peter Drucker's life. His relentlessly curious mind was active throughout his long life and drove the work he did. One of the main ways he learned was by teaching, and it's a benefit many of us can profitably consider.

For knowledge workers, teaching and learning present many options for getting involved, making a difference, and providing personal growth and self-development. They are a cornerstone of living in more than one world, because they involve you in something outside of your regular job, where you meet and work with people different from you and your regular associates. They also provide a platform for personal growth.

Either activity can be a crucial part of your Total Life List, and one that will affect other parts of your list. For instance, if you teach as a volunteer, you may gain benefits in both the teaching/learning and volunteerism categories. The people with whom you interact may be added to the list in the categories of friends or professional colleagues. Teaching especially gives you opportunities to make society a better place.

In teaching, you may have opportunities to further the personal development of other people that you may not have in your regular job. In some cases, you can still teach and learn as part of your regular job. Knowledge workers are often involved in teaching classes or providing training within the workplace. If you work for a large enough organization, there are usually continuous opportunities for either taking classes on-site, or regular training. Some workplaces also provide tuition assistance toward graduate degrees.

Other learning opportunities are available at workshops, seminars, and annual meetings of professional associations. (These also provide teaching opportunities.) Learning new things on a regular basis feeds into Drucker's cherished idea of building on your strengths and minimizing your weaknesses. You can build on your strengths by incorporating continuous learning into what you do, and you can minimize your weaknesses by learning enough to do reasonably well at something that isn't necessarily part of your core competencies, and is unlikely to become so.

A hallmark of Drucker's tough yet realistic and encouraging style is to say, for example, that you might not be a born mathematician, but you can learn enough about math to apply it when needed. Knowing about a variety of subjects, in his view, helps knowledge workers understand what their colleagues are trying to do and say. Drucker stressed the importance of communication and responsibility between colleagues at work. He also emphasized that learning beyond your own discipline is crucial to effective communication and part of the responsible oversight of information you owe to others. In this information age, people and ideas are connected as never before.

Drucker's intellectual curiosity was one of the factors that kept his mind active and alive into extreme old age. It helped him remain relevant and enabled him to write books even after turning ninety. As life spans increase, many knowledge workers will have similar needs for relevancy, as we work longer and seek more intellectually challenging retirement years. More people are moving to university towns after retirement, partly for the ability to take classes at reduced rates. More schools are opening their doors for "University for a Day" classes, where members of the public pay a relatively small fee for a day's worth of lectures from their faculty. What subjects are you curious to learn about? What do you feel you can teach to others?

Continuous Learning

Knowledge workers expect continuous learning and continuous training.[68]

DRUCKER SAID THAT ONE of the three things that attracts and retains volunteers in nonprofit organizations is continuous learning. One way to interpret this is that volunteers pick the particular subject or cause to which they want to contribute, and want opportunities to learn about this subject or cause as they grow in their role as a volunteer. This extends beyond the benefits nonprofits can provide to any sort of work situation. As noted in the previous section, many employers do provide continuous learning opportunities, probably even more than one person can handle in any given year. However, if you are dissatisfied with the learning opportunities on your job—and perhaps there aren't any you find relevant—volunteering where you are given those opportunities can be an important educational resource.

But it's up to individual knowledge workers to figure out how to incorporate continuous learning as a natural part of their daily life. This means determining your priorities, deciding what you'd like to learn and how you'll learn it, and figuring out how to build in the time to accommodate learning. For many people, this will involve a blend of formal classes and self-directed learning from reading books and articles, finding relevant material online, and learning by direct observation or asking other people. How do you learn best? Would you say your best learning takes place in the classroom, through your own reading, or on the job? What holds you back from deeper learning experiences?

In Drucker's vision of a strong, functioning society, education always had a key role. Knowledge workers must start learning during their formal schooling and never stop throughout their lives. They must develop, beyond a subject knowledge, the *ability to learn*. Knowledge is always becoming obsolete, and new subjects continually emerge.

Drucker noted that learning has to be not just continuous—especially on the job—but lifelong as well. Learning should be considered a source of satisfaction and even pleasure, rather than a duty. Since our society and its institutions are now built around knowledge and information, lifelong learning is an obvious cornerstone for this type of building. Drucker also knew that more people had to become convinced of this point of view, and that we have not yet sold the concept in an organized way. If our institutions are truly organized for constant change, workers have to embody this same outlook.

Some professions, such as medicine, require practitioners to earn continuing educational credits on an ongoing basis and to keep up with new techniques and concepts. Surely we would feel uneasy with our doctors or dentists if they weren't up to speed on the latest knowledge their professions have to offer.

Fortunately, the opportunities are boundless for knowledge worker education, particularly in our online age. Community colleges and courses offered by local towns and cities present other ways to acquire or refine new skills, or try out new areas of interest.

Relatively informal learning opportunities abound at such venues as:

» Industry and professional conferences
» Trade shows
» Seminars
» Online Web seminars
» Lectures open to the public at local universities
» Author appearances at bookstores and schools
» "Brown bag" events at workplaces and other settings

The Web sites of schools throughout the world present informal learning opportunities through online research, lecture notes, syllabi, bibliographies, and so on. Some of these sites, plus others from noneducational institutions, offer podcasts of lectures and educational programs.

In the quotation about "learning institutions" that

opens this chapter, Drucker gives a nod to Peter Senge's formulation of "the learning organization," the basis of Senge's influential 1990 book, *The Fifth Discipline*. In Senge's vision, this type of organization coalesces and evolves through its members engaging in five interrelated disciplines: Personal Mastery, Mental Models, Building Shared Vision, Team Learning, and Systems Thinking (the Fifth Discipline). Senge writes that these are "organizations where people continually expand their capacity to create the results they truly desire, where new and expansive patterns of thinking are nurtured, where collective aspiration is set free, and where people are continually learning how to learn together."[69] Senge and Drucker later collaborated in 2001 on a video and accompanying workbook, *Leading in a Time of Change: A Conversation with Peter F. Drucker and Peter M. Senge*. Although it is not about learning, it still may be of interest to people who are curious about the interaction of two first-rate minds on an important topic.

Corporations have evidently gotten the message about lifelong development. They have made big investments in training of all types—particularly in computer hardware and software. Some organizations now have Chief Learning Officers. These people are responsible for the educational and training programs of the organization, including those for high-level executives. These officers design curricula, arrange for teachers and speakers, and may arrange for online learning opportunities. In this way, they help members of the organizations learn about some of the subjects that will be crucial to them in meeting the challenges of the future.

Many corporations have well-developed in-house

learning programs, such as McDonald's Hamburger University, Motorola University, and the famous General Electric management development institution in Croton-on-Hudson, New York. The latter became well known in the days when Jack Welch was CEO and personally taught some of the classes. It is now named in his honor as the John F. Welch Leadership Development Center. These in-house universities teach more elaborate and involved courses than just isolated classes or training periods. They often deal in subjects such as leadership and advanced management techniques, more so than, for instance, learning new software programs, or how to use particular types of computer hardware. (The latter subjects are certainly important, and this type of learning is still crucial within organizations.)

You may want to consider earning an advanced degree. For people in the business community, this might be an MBA (Master of Business Administration). Executives who may or may not have an MBA, but who have more senior level experience, can now choose from many executive management MBAs, a degree that Drucker pioneered in the 1970s during his early years teaching at Claremont. Getting an MBA or another type of graduate degree can be valuable in a number of ways. Beyond what you learn, you can become part of a powerful network of alumni who can help open doors and provide opportunities. You may be able to command a higher salary and a more influential position where you work or elsewhere.

Obtaining any kind of graduate degree is a serious decision that should be thought through and discussed with family members. There may be expense involved, and hefty student loans that must be repaid. You should have clear goals and reasons for embarking on this type of learning journey, which could be a long one. Those thinking about the MBA path may want to read Mark Albion's 2008 book, *More than Money: Questions Every MBA Needs to Answer.*

Many universities offer short-term programs in leadership, marketing, financial management, and more, many with a global focus. The range and possibilities of these programs can be seen in the back pages of the British news weekly *The Economist*, one of Drucker's favorite publications. You are likely to see a number of advertisements for on-site and online programs from such geographically diverse schools as Harvard, Oxford, the University of Amsterdam, and the IESE Business School at the University of Navarra in Spain.

ASK YOURSELF

Do I consciously build continuous learning into my life? When I attend conferences and trade shows, do I have a strategy ahead of time for making the most of learning opportunities, such as how I choose which classes to attend, and what I hope to learn?

In addition to earning online degrees, there are many online courses people can take, working at their own pace. Drucker worked with the e-learning company Corpedia to develop online learning modules. Drucker said that he spent considerable time coming up with the right sort of format for these courses. He was aware that such courses required a different mindset for the student, and couldn't be a simple replication of the classroom experience. In

Even though Drucker advocated that knowledge workers return to the classroom periodically, the paradox is that Drucker didn't do this himself, at least not formally. After he earned a doctorate in international law at Germany's Frankfurt University in 1931, he didn't earn other degrees. Granted, a doctorate is the highest degree you can get. Yet he could have enrolled in other formal degree programs in different subjects, and didn't do so. He had other ways of building continuous learning into his life that revolved around his own teaching, his prodigious reading and search for knowledge, and his personal contacts with highly accomplished people.

online courses, you would be not part of a class where you would interact in person with a professor and classmates, but instead would learn completely on your own, which involves a different mental approach. (It's important to note, however, that some online courses do provide for Web-based or telephone-based interaction with teacher and classmates.) Drucker also believed that the changing nature of teaching to more computer-based involvement would change the results of the learning process for many people. One big reason is that the computer is patient and impersonal. A student may feel less rushed and pressured in learning when interacting with a computer program, rather than with a professor and classmates. Those who have trouble learning the traditional way may find they are much better students under the new methods, while people who thrive under the current system may find the new order more challenging.

Knowledge Workers as Teachers

Knowledge work requires continuous learning on the part of the knowledge worker, but equally continuous teaching on the part of the knowledge worker.[70]

KNOWLEDGE WORKERS HAVE AMPLE opportunities to take advantage of the benefits of teaching in a variety of formal and informal settings. This could include adjunct teaching at local universities, teaching online classes offered by many universities, giving presentations at work and at conferences, volunteer teaching at your place of worship, tutoring, making presentations to professional societies and associations, or guiding internships. The best teachers change the lives of their students for the better. Knowledge workers who want to see tangible results or benefits of their work may find gratification in teaching.

If you don't currently teach but are interested in getting started, it's best to consider the kinds of opportunities open to you: check with possible schools, places of worship, professional associations, and your own workplace to start. If you know people who teach similar classes, ask them how they got started, and whom you would need to contact to find out more. While you'd need some sort of professional certification to teach in elementary or high schools, you generally won't need this for teaching in universities. But it's possible you'll need an academic degree related to what you'd like to teach.

Teaching and training opportunities could be available in the kind of in-house corporate programs mentioned in the previous section. This kind of experience can lead to more formal teaching elsewhere. Many people find rewarding teaching opportunities at their place of worship, which helps them meet new people, learn new subjects, and learn more about what they already know.

Knowledge workers, Drucker claimed, often learn the most when teaching. By teaching your fellow professionals, you can boost your productivity and performance. It forces you to continually keep up with your subject, and learn how to communicate it to others. Teaching gives knowledge workers a setting for organizing knowledge logically, in ways they may not have considered.

Another benefit of teaching is meeting and working with a completely different group of people from your usual colleagues. In addition

ASK YOURSELF

If I currently teach, what benefits does it bring to other areas of my life? What are the accompanying drawbacks and challenges? If I am interested in teaching, who can guide me in the right direction? How can I incorporate teaching— formally or informally—into my life?

to meeting students, you may invite guest speakers, lecturers, and panelists to address your class. This can add to your personal networks and enrich your life. Or you may deliver a guest lecture or appear as a panelist in someone else's class—an excellent way to "get your feet wet" teaching.

People who develop second or parallel careers as teachers often have the revelation of realizing a talent they never suspected they had. Teaching forces you to deal with people in different ways, and requires management of a classroom and students. This can be a benefit for people who want to build some management activities into their lives, but don't want to be a full-time manager within an organization. For the length of a semester, a class must be managed, during class time and outside of it. Time must be managed well, in class and outside. In today's environment, teachers increasingly must make themselves available to students, especially through e-mail. Grades must be determined, papers and exams read, lesson plans and lectures prepared, and so on. You have to hold each student accountable for attaining the goals of your course. When it all comes together, there will be tremendous benefits for both teacher and students.

Teaching also forces you to think differently and to present ideas in ways you may not have previously considered. For example, you may begin as a teacher with a lecture-oriented approach in the classroom. But because so many of today's students are visually oriented, you may

---

DRUCKER'S LIFE AND WORK

Drucker was a master teacher who forged a deep bond with his students, many of whom he stayed in touch with for many years afterwards. He learned a lot from these people—especially those who were in the advanced executive MBA program, because they had a lot of experience in particular industries. As a professor, Drucker spent a lot of time on his students. He did not use teaching assistants. He read all papers three times before assigning a grade, and would allow students to rewrite their papers in hopes of getting an A. For an in-depth portrait of Drucker as a professor, you might enjoy William A. Cohen's 2008 book, *A Class with Drucker: The Lost Lessons of the World's Greatest Management Teacher*. Cohen was Drucker's first Ph.D. student at the Drucker School in the 1970s.

learn to get across your ideas in a more visual way, with pictures and graphics, and less bullet-point-laden Power-Point presentations. In addition, powerful and easy-to-use course management software from companies such as Blackboard allow teachers to incorporate technology in a meaningful and time-saving way.

Drucker's wide-ranging experience as a consultant, author, and professor helped him to be an effective instructor, because he could incorporate experiences from his work with organizations, managers, and leaders into his teaching. Most knowledge workers will not have Drucker's depth of experience, but may have enough to make an important contribution to some area of teaching. If you are an adjunct professor, for instance, you not only experience another world, but also bring your own part of the outside world to your students and new colleagues. Adjuncts (who also might have similar titles such as lecturers) are part-time faculty members in universities who are not on a tenure track, and who usually don't have some of the formal responsibilities of full-time professors, such as advising students.

Any kind of teaching is challenging, and should not be initiated lightly. Time can be a problem. You may not be able to teach year-round. And while it's beneficial to learn new things because you are teaching, it takes time, and that time will have to come from somewhere. It's also beneficial to learn new forms of technology that come with teaching, but again a learning curve must be factored in to your schedule. Finally, the flip side of the benefit of working with new people may be that students or others may behave in ways that confront you with the challenge of resolving difficult issues and dealing with situations you'd rather not face!

The Odyssey Experience

During a visit to the Drucker-Ito School in 2008, I was deeply moved by an exhibit about a course taught at the school the year before by Charles and Elizabeth Handy. I asked Charles for a description of the course, which I feel is highly relevant to readers of this book. This is his response.

Images often speak louder than words. At least that is what we found when we discussed with people what really mattered in their lives. My wife, Elizabeth, a talented portrait photographer, and I had been experimenting with what we called still life portraits. We suggested to individuals and couples who had commissioned portraits of themselves that, in addition to a photograph of their person, they should select five objects and one flower that together represented who they were and what mattered most to them. Arranged on a table, these were then photographed by Elizabeth to become modern versions of the old Dutch still life paintings. The resulting pictures were always pleasing to the eye, making the point that all lives can be made beautiful, with a little thought and determination.

Invited to teach a course at the Drucker School of Management in Claremont while on sabbatical, we decided to use this process to help individuals first to reflect on their priorities in their life's journey, what we described as their Odyssey experience. We went further and next asked them to compose still life portraits for their organizations in the present and then, third, for their organizations as they would like them to be. The portraits by themselves said little until they were explained and the deeper meanings of the objects revealed. The more the ten individuals in the course spoke of their chosen objects to us and the other members of the group, the deeper they went until they had shared the full richness of their lives and their work as they saw them unfolding.

The course lasted five weeks with two mornings of meetings each week. At the end, because there is no one right way to describe a life, we dispensed with grades and instead arranged an exhibition in the entrance hall of the school and celebrated the end of the course with an open invitation to the opening of our makeshift gallery, to which families, professors, and even the university president came. It was a joyous occasion, one that we felt Peter Drucker would have appreciated, because it emphasized the essential humanity of organizations and the meaning that people seek in their work and life. For us, the teachers, it was the most satisfying course that either of us has ever experienced. Six months later, the gallery is still in place, we continue to be in touch with several of the students, and the Drucker School is now using the Still Life as part of the induction process for the whole of its executive program.

Charles and Elizabeth Handy

Charles describes himself nowadays as a social philosopher; he has worked as an oil executive, a business school professor, and in BBC broadcasting, and is widely acknowledged as a world leader in management thinking. Elizabeth has been a freelance interior designer, a marriage guidance counselor, and is now a distinguished portrait photographer. She embarked on her third career in her late forties and got her photography degree on the same day as her son got his at Cambridge. The Handys have, in recent years, collaborated on several books, most notably *The New Alchemists* and *Reinvented Lives: Women at Sixty*.

Learning How to Learn

If you haven't learned how to learn, you'll have a hard time. Knowing how to learn is partly curiosity. But it's also a discipline.[71]

DRUCKER DEVELOPED A SELF-STUDY system in which every few years he picked a new topic and studied it intensively on his own. In the years immediately preceding his death, perhaps realizing that because of his age a three-year system was impractical, he accelerated the projects into three-month time frames. In 2002, in the months before his ninety-third birthday, he was re-reading all of Shakespeare's plays while consulting Harold Bloom's literary guide. Perhaps, knowing he probably didn't have many years to live, he wanted to study the highest reaches literature has to offer. Since this was self-directed learning, he had a choice of any subject. What would we pick, given a similar situation? How many of us have read all of Shakespeare's plays, let alone re-read them?

For Drucker, potential learning from anything and everything was built into the fabric of his being. It was one of the factors contributing to his extreme success. And it's something that anyone with the sufficient desire and motivation can emulate. No matter how many months or years it takes, the system holds promise for today's knowledge worker. If you don't have the time or inclination for formal classes or degrees, you can still pick subjects and find more than enough material in print and online. You will also learn that in studying one subject, you are bound to learn about others, and how they connect and interrelate. And if you don't like what you're studying, you can drop it and pick something else. Drucker said there were times that he found himself growing bored months into a self-study program. When that happened, he cut his losses by dropping that program and starting a new one.

ASK YOURSELF

Have I thought about designing a self-study system based on a combination of printed and online material? Do I learn better by reading, listening, writing, or teaching—or some combination of these areas?

Related to learning how to learn is being aware of how you learn. Drucker believed this was a key element in self-management. Some people, he said, were primarily readers and others primarily listeners. In many cases, we learn by doing—either by learning on the job from our colleagues and daily experiences, or in apprenticeships, or by simply learning about a problem, issue, or skill as we tackle it. Many people prefer to talk to an expert or a colleague, especially if it is something quick related to a computer. Others are happy to find the same knowledge by reading a book, a manual, or online Web instructions.

Even though Drucker was a professor, he learned the most not from formal classes or other professors, but from his teaching, writing, and from direct contact with other people. He learned a lot from his clients and his former bosses. It's instructive to think that Drucker gave this subject of learning so much attention over the years. When he discussed his seven formative experiences in the book *Drucker on Asia*, none of the learning experiences was based in a classroom. They came from such disparate sources as libraries, the world of opera, the Jesuits, and his editor-in-chief when he was a young journalist in Germany.

Working with Knowledge, Information, and Data

Knowledge is always embodied in a person; carried by a person; created, augmented, or improved by a person; applied by a person; taught and passed on by a person; used or misused by a person. The shift to the knowledge society therefore puts the person in the center.[72]

THE RAW MATERIALS OF teaching and learning are knowledge and its stepping stones, information and data. Peter Drucker began writing about knowledge workers in the 1957 book *Landmarks of Tomorrow*. He put the spotlight on knowledge and its importance to accomplishing the work of the late twentieth and early twenty-first centuries, much as he had done earlier with his focus on the practice of management.

He warned that today's knowledge workers would have to know how to organize their information. "In the past," Drucker said, "we always had a desperate shortage of information. Now we have an incredible overload of data.

And the executive of tomorrow will have to learn how to transform data into information, which very few know."[73] Since the terms *data* and *information* are often used incorrectly as interchangeable, it helps to think about the difference between the two, and the relation of each to knowledge.

Data are the kernels of what eventually may become knowledge, but require increasing levels of understanding as they are first transformed into information. Once information progresses further and is put to use, it then becomes knowledge. Understanding this continuum from data to information to knowledge helps give you a framework for understanding your work. It might be helpful to think of the stock tables in newspapers. If you look at the numbers and words in the tables without connecting them to any other kind of information or knowledge, you are looking at data. If you look at the rows of numbers and understand that you are looking at stock numbers for General Electric, you have now moved into the realm of information. If you understand those numbers, and can make connections to what you know about stocks, the stock market, the company, and the industry, you now have knowledge that can—if you choose—be used for a decision on whether to buy or sell the stock.

In 1990, Drucker wrote in *The Economist* (later reprinted in his collection *Managing for the Future*): "But data is not information. Information is data endowed with relevance and purpose. A company must decide what information it needs to operate its affairs, otherwise it will drown in data."[74] Note that this was written when major databases such as LexisNexis existed, but before the World Wide Web. If we felt we were drowning in data before the Web, that seems like the good old days now! It's not only companies that are in danger of drowning in data. The same is true for individuals, whether they work in companies or alone.

Drucker's view of data and information echoed his belief in the importance of the external world. In order to learn new information and transform it into knowledge, we have to go outside ourselves, to other people as well as to online and printed sources. By consulting these sources, we learn what is going on beyond our own four walls, and what it means to us.

For Drucker, knowledge existed in its application, by putting it to work. It must be learned to begin with, and either remembered or accessed to be put to good use. He didn't discount the pleasure and satisfaction of learning for its own sake, but he liked to focus on practical applications, especially those that held benefits for other people. Whether we are teaching, learning, or working, he gave us a lot to consider about how knowledge can be used in the most productive ways. He was a master of getting to the heart of the matter, and finding the most relevant pieces of data or information, which could then be transformed into knowledge. This has become increasingly important as we face so many competing sources of information, especially online.

Drucker laid out some first principles of knowledge work and the knowledge society on May 4, 1994, in the prestigious Edwin L. Godkin Lecture at the John F. Kennedy School of Government of Harvard University. Although he had no way of knowing it at the time, the knowledge world was about to undergo a huge shift. The World Wide Web had recently been introduced, but was not yet in widespread use. It was more than four years before Google, but some search engines and directories such as Yahoo! were beginning to appear.

The key knowledge principles advanced in his lecture are:

» Continuous learning is necessary.
» The acquisition and application of knowledge is increasingly important as a competitive factor for individuals, organizations, industries, and countries.
» In the knowledge society, leadership is open to any individual.
» The availability of knowledge means hypercompetition for individuals, organizations, industries, and countries.
» Theoretical knowledge is not enough.
» Knowledge work requires making yourself understood by others, and the ability to learn how to integrate the specialized knowledge of others with your own.
» Knowledge workers need access to an organization to fulfill their work.
» There is no hierarchy of knowledge; whatever knowledge fits the situation is the right knowledge at the time.

Knowledge was the foundation of all of Drucker's work. He was a master at finding what was relevant in any given situation and communicating it to his readers or students. Although he wrote about technology and its importance for data, information, and knowledge, he didn't use a computer. He wrote on a typewriter and found information in a number of different ways: through the prodigious skills of his wife, Doris; from the continual reading of many books, newspapers, and magazines; and from the use of libraries. He also had another valuable advantage: numerous friends, colleagues, and others would send him things they had just published or were working on, putting him in the privileged position of receiving nascent information.

Most of what Drucker said about working with knowledge and information holds true today, and we can see it through the lens of all the technological breakthroughs that have come since. He talked about the shift from farming and blue-collar, industrial, manual workers to knowledge workers, and the career choices now available to so many people, who were no longer restricted to following in their parents' footsteps. Knowledge workers, he claimed, had become the leading class of society, if not its ruling class.

What makes a knowledge worker? First of all, it is formal education, and often many years of it. It is the kind of work that can't be learned through apprenticeship, which was prevalent in previous centuries. It's a mistake to think that knowledge workers succeed solely on their brainpower. Drucker noted that skill in working with one's hands is crucial to, for instance, a neurosurgeon. But manual dexterity alone will not qualify someone for this career. Formal schooling, knowledge, and experience are required, along with the manual requirements.

Despite the drastic changes we have seen because of the Internet since 1994, Drucker's ideas and principles continue to hold up well. The pace of technological change is even more breathtaking now, which makes it especially difficult for managers who are expected to mold the knowledge society, and the knowledge-based organizations they are entrusted to run. As Drucker pointed out, the emergence of the knowledge society presents both threats and opportunities for the individual knowledge worker. All the more reason to remember his emphasis on capitalizing on opportunities.

Chapter Question Summaries

Continuous Learning Think about the extent to which you consciously build continuous learning into your life, and whether you have strategies for making the most of learning opportunities at conferences, trade shows, and similar events.

Knowledge Workers as Teachers If you are already teaching, think about the benefits you receive from it, as well as some of the drawbacks and challenges. If you are interested in teaching, think about who could help you get started, and how you can contact them.

Learning How to Learn Consider the possibility of a self-study system similar to the ones Drucker devised for himself, and how much you'd rely on printed or online material. Also think about your learning styles, and whether you learn best by reading, writing, listening, teaching others, or a combination of some or all of these methods.

Working with Knowledge, Information, and Data Think about the information you need to perform your job, including where it comes from and how you find it. Also think about how you integrate your specialized knowledge with that of your colleagues.

Chapter Recap and Next Steps

In this chapter we have looked at the twin subjects of teaching and learning. We've seen how important they were to Drucker throughout his life, and how they can enrich your own life. We have covered:

» Opportunities for continuous, lifelong learning, inside and outside of your daily employment
» The benefits of teaching, including ways to start investigating formal and informal teaching opportunities
» How you can apply Drucker's three-year self-study system for your own benefit
» Drucker's key principles of working with and organizing information, and transforming that information into useful knowledge

In the conclusion of this book, we'll briefly recap the learning journey we've been on, and how you can take its lessons into the future.

Hints for Creating Your Total Life List

When considering how to incorporate teaching and learning into your life, it's helpful to think of the different categories these activities fall into on your Total Life List. Some of the possibilities include:

1. and 2. Immediate and Extended family (Family members can take classes together, especially in areas such as continuing education and courses in religious institutions. In addition, family members can teach together, as in the Charles and Elizabeth Handy example above.)
3. Closer work colleagues (people you'll meet and interact with if you start teaching)
4. Friends (people you'll meet through both teaching and learning)
5. People in your various professional networks (those you'll add by both teaching and learning)
6. Various places of current employment (added through teaching and learning)
7. Professional affiliations and associations (added through teaching and learning)
8. Ongoing learning activities
9. Teaching
10. Volunteer activities (added through teaching)
11. Work with nonprofit organizations, or social entrepreneurship (added through teaching)
12. Mentoring (added through teaching)
13. Outside interests of all types, including areas such as sports leagues, amateur interest societies, religious/ spiritual activities or study, book groups, or creative

areas such as writing, art, or playing music (through both teaching and learning)

14. Exercise and other mind-body activities (through both teaching and learning)

Exercise: The guest lecture

Prepare a "guest lecture," in PowerPoint or some other organized form, based on the work you do, for an imagined course on your subject. If you were to be speaking for 15 to 30 minutes, what would you tell the class about how your work is done, and what information you require to do it well?

You can broaden this to include a sample bibliography of online and printed sources about your profession and place of work. What questions will you need to ask yourself to give your students a solid understanding of the importance of your work? Think of the preparation you'll need in anticipating their questions. How will you organize your material? You can prepare a handout, possibly based on the notes for your PowerPoint, if you choose to use that format.

This exercise will give you a start on approaching teaching fundamentals, and will also help you see the work you do in a new light.

Launching Your Journey

Although we have come to the end of our reading journey in *Living in More Than One World*, ideally you will consider this a new beginning in your life. The Total Life List featured in each chapter is meant to be a living, breathing document that will change as your own circumstances evolve. By working on it as often as you can, you develop a vivid sense of where your life is now personally and professionally, and where you'd like it to be.

You've now considered what it means to live a multifaceted life, and what the components of that life may entail. You've considered some of the possible challenges and pitfalls, as well as the benefits. As often as possible, there have been concrete suggestions along the way to help you decide about areas you'd like to add (or subtract) from your life.

The following brief recap gives you an overview of what a multidimensional life might consist of for you. Here are some of the main areas we've explored:

- » Creating a multifaceted life, including developing serious outside interests (Chapter 1)
- » How core competencies help you get the most out of being multidimensional (Chapter 2)
- » Parallel careers (Chapter 3)
- » Second careers (Chapter 3)
- » Personal reinvention (Chapter 3)
- » Volunteerism, social entrepreneurship, servant leadership, and related areas (Chapter 4)
- » Teaching (Chapter 5)
- » Continuous, lifelong learning (Chapter 5)

The Total Life List at the end of each chapter reflects and amplifies each of the themes covered. If you haven't had time to add to it as you've read, you can now go back and fill in the names of people and activities of the present and the future. You may find that after reading the entire book, you want to make some changes to your initial list. It is a good idea to reconsider your list periodically and see if it really reflects you as the person you are now.

For instance, if you are undergoing a personal reinvention, discussed in Chapter 3, it is bound to affect many of the fourteen categories of the list. If you are regularly practicing Drucker's concept of systematic/planned abandonment (covered in Chapter 2), this will also affect on many of the areas.

This book will have served its purpose if you consider yourself, the work you do, and your relationships with other people in a new light. You may now see something of Drucker in yourself. Whatever it is, think about how to put it to use, for your own benefit and especially for the benefit of other people.

We will all live in a better world if enough people act

on the principles described in this book. We'll see benefits as friends, family members, and colleagues if people make the most of their talents, learn as much as possible and share that knowledge, and extend their generosity in many different settings. The current era is a challenging, even wrenching time for knowledge workers. We all need a sense of hope, backed by solid strategies of what to do to create a better tomorrow.

After reading so many of Peter Drucker's quotes and ideas, your appetite may be whetted to read more of his work. At the end of this book is a brief, annotated reading list of some of his most important books that dovetail with the themes of *Living in More Than One World.* As an author, Drucker was prodigious. His publications will keep you busy for years to come, if you are so inclined. As you read his material, consider how it relates to the principles outlined in *Living in More Than One World,* and what ideas and inspirations Drucker continues to give you for your Total Life List. Be patient, but persistent. Good luck on your continued journey!

With more than forty books published by Peter Drucker since 1939, the task of selecting ones to read can be challenging. One shortcut is to read the annotated bibliography prepared by Drucker's colleague Joseph A. Maciariello, which has appeared in both *The Daily Drucker* and *Management: Revised Edition*.

Maciariello's bibliography provides a handy paragraph on each book, and is a worthy guide. But here I provide a different type of guide, approaching Drucker's vast body of writings by theme, so you can quickly discern which ones will be of immediate interest. Consider this a starting point on your Drucker reading journey.

The Quickest Route to Drucker's Books

The Daily Drucker (2004) has become quite popular. Although most of its material had been published previously, the book contains added material from both Drucker and Maciariello. These book excerpts are presented in a topic-a-day format, giving it a somewhat inspirational aura. The book makes a great gift. In the back, you'll find a section called "Readings by Topic." You may want to concentrate at first on some of the individual-oriented topics, such as "Knowledge Workers" or "Managing Oneself."

The Essential Drucker (2001) includes writings from various books, focusing on management for the organization, the individual, and society. While not as user-friendly as *The Daily Drucker,* it is still worth owning for both serious Drucker devotees and newer fans of his work.

The Most Crucial and Comprehensive Drucker Books on Management

Management: Revised Edition (2008) is the revised and up-dated version of *Management: Tasks, Responsibilities, Practices* (1973). If you become a serious reader, you'll want both editions, since a lot was dropped for the 2008 book (more than two hundred pages). For a stimulating over-view of Drucker's thoughts on how to lead a more mean-ingful and fulfilling life, read chapter 45 of *Management: Revised Edition*, "Managing Oneself," which originally ap-peared in the 1999 book *Management Challenges for the 21st Century*.

The Practice of Management (1954) marks the invention of modern management, according to Jack Beatty, who wrote *The World According to Peter Drucker*. Parts of *The Practice of Management* can seem dated, but many readers consider it a classic.

The Effective Executive (1967) is one of Drucker's biggest-selling books and a steady seller year after year. This was his first book to focus on the individual, broadening the focus beyond management. For a strong statement on self-development, read the final chapter, "Conclusion: Effectiveness Must Be Learned," which is less than ten pages long. It's worth getting the 2006 paperback reissue for the inclusion of his long article from the June 2004 issue of *Harvard Business Review*, "What Makes an Effective Executive?"

The Effective Executive in Action (2006) was published shortly after Drucker's death. It is in a workbook format, with sections of the original book from forty years earlier, which still hold up well. It is supplemented by follow-up questions and actions, with space for the reader to write responses and reflections.

The subjects of *Innovation and Entrepreneurship* (1985) are hot topics today, with many books on each discipline, but that was not the case at the time Drucker wrote this book. Though some of the examples are dated, it is well worth reading, and continues to be a strong seller.

Managing the Non-Profit Organization (1990 and 2005) spotlights management of nonprofits of all types, including hospitals, churches, and schools. It includes interviews conducted by Drucker with such luminaries as Frances Hesselbein (about her leadership of the Girl Scouts) and Dudley Hafner (then executive vice president and CEO of the American Heart Association). You may enjoy the short final chapters of each section called "Summary: The Action Implications." It is a concise guide to self-development and self-renewal that is applicable beyond the nonprofit world.

Drucker Books on Society

The New Realities (1989) and *Post-Capitalist Society* (1993) are wonderful works of original material on societal issues, including business, government, and education. The books still seem fresh and thought-provoking today. The final chapters of *Post-Capitalist Society,* "Knowledge: Its Economics and Its Productivity," "The Accountable School," and "The Educated Person" provide a strong underpinning for the concepts discussed in Chapter 5 of this book.

The Ecological Vision: Reflections on the American Condition (1993) packs a lot of material into 466 pages. Although there is much about society in general, these essays include several chapters on business and technology. Of particular interest are two highly personal essays that close the book, "The Unfashionable Kierkegaard," and "Reflections of a Social Ecologist."

Drucker on Drucker

Adventures of a Bystander (1978; the 1998 edition contains a new preface by Drucker) is the closest Drucker came to writing his memoirs. In it, he looks at his life through stories about other people and his relationship to them. The highly personal style is endearing. Of particular interest are sections on his friendships with Marshall McLuhan and R. Buckminster Fuller before each became a famous cultural icon. The 1990 book *Managing the Non-Profit Organization* also has fascinating sections about Drucker's life.

Final Thoughts on Drucker's Books

This reader's guide has skipped a number of Drucker's books, including most of the anthologies of his writings (other than *The Essential Drucker* and *The Ecological Vision*). But all of his books are worth reading. A few books are out of print, but in the information-rich world in which we now live, many of these should be relatively easy to obtain on the Web, or at used bookstores. Many libraries are well stocked with Drucker's works. It is a tribute to the timelessness of his message that so many of his books are so readily available.

Further Reading

Books by Peter F. Drucker

Drucker, Peter F. *Adventures of a Bystander*. New York: Harper & Row, 1978; revised ed., New York: John Wiley & Sons, 1998.

———. *The Daily Drucker: 366 Days of Insight and Motivation for Getting the Right Things Done*. New York: Harper-Business, 2004.

———. *The Ecological Vision: Reflections on the American Condition*. New Brunswick, N.J.: Transaction Publishers, 1993.

———. *The Effective Executive*. New York: Harper & Row, 1967; revised ed., New York: Collins, 2006.

———. *The Effective Executive in Action: A Journal for Getting the Right Things Done*. New York: Collins, 2006.

———. *The Essential Drucker: The Best of Sixty Years of Peter*

Drucker's Essential Writings on Management. New York: HarperBusiness, 2001.

———. *Innovation and Entrepreneurship: Practice and Principles*. New York: Harper & Row, 1985.

———, with Joseph A. Maciariello. *Management: Revised Edition*. New York: Collins, 2008.

———. *Management: Tasks, Responsibilities, Practices*. New York: Harper & Row, 1973.

———. *Managing the Non-Profit Organization: Practices and Principles*. New York: HarperCollins, 1990.

———. *The New Realities: In Government and Politics, in Economics and Business, in Society and World View*. New York: Harper & Row, 1989.

———. *Post-Capitalist Society*. New York: HarperBusiness, 1993.

———. *The Practice of Management:* New York: Harper & Row, 1954.

Books by Other Authors

Books mentioned in the text are listed here.

Albion, Mark. *Making a Life, Making a Living: Reclaiming Your Purpose and Passion in Business and in Life*. New York: Warner Business Books, 2000.

———. *More than Money: Questions Every MBA Needs to Answer*. San Francisco: Berrett-Koehler, 2008.

Beatty, Jack. *The World According to Peter Drucker*. New York: Free Press, 1998.

Bornstein, David. *How to Change the World: Social Entrepreneurs and the Power of New Ideas*. 2004; updated ed., New York: Oxford University Press, 2007.

———. *The Price of a Dream: The Story of the Grameen Bank and the Idea That Is Helping the Poor to Change Their Lives.* New York: Simon & Schuster, 1996.

Bronson, Po. *What Should I Do With My Life? The True Story of People Who Answered the Ultimate Question.* Updated ed., New York: Random House, 2003.

Buford, Bob. *Halftime: Changing Your Game Plan from Success to Significance.* Grand Rapids, Mich.: Zondervan, 1994; revised ed., *Halftime: Moving from Success to Significance.* Grand Rapids, Mich.: Zondervan, 2009.

———. *Stuck in Halftime: Reinvesting Your One and Only Life.* Grand Rapids, Mich.: Zondervan, 2001.

———. *Finishing Well: What People Who Really Live Do Differently!* Nashville, Tenn.: Integrity, 2004.

Cohen, William A. *A Class with Drucker: The Lost Lessons of the World's Greatest Management Teacher.* New York: AMACOM, American Management Association, 2008.

Collins, Jim. *Good to Great.* New York: HarperBusiness, 2001.

De Pree, Max. *Leadership Is an Art.* 1989; revised ed., New York: Broadway Business, 2004.

———. *Leadership Jazz.* 1991; revised ed., New York: Broadway Business, 2008.

Drucker, Doris. *Invent Radium or I'll Pull Your Hair.* Chicago: University of Chicago Press, 2004.

Friedman, Thomas L. *The World Is Flat: A Brief History of the Twenty-First Century.* 2005; 2nd revised ed., New York: Picador/Farrar, Straus and Giroux, 2007.

Greenleaf, Robert K. *On Becoming a Servant Leader.* San Francisco: Jossey-Bass, 1996.

———. *Servant Leadership: A Journey into the Nature of Legitimate Power and Greatness.* 25th anniversary ed., Mahwah, N.J.: Paulist Press, 2002.

Hamel, Gary, and C. K. Prahalad. *Competing for the Future.* Boston: Harvard Business School Press, 1994; revised ed., 2006.

Kanter, Rosabeth Moss. *America the Principled: 6 Opportunities for Becoming a Can-Do Nation Once Again.* New York: Crown Publishers, 2007.

Raynolds, John, with Gene Stone. *The Halo Effect: How Volunteering to Help Others Can Lead to a Better Career and a More Fulfilling Life.* New York: Golden Books Adult Publishing, 1998.

Senge, Peter M. *The Fifth Discipline: The Art and Practice of the Learning Organization.* New York: Currency Doubleday, 1990; revised ed., New York: Broadway Business, 2006.

Shore, Bill. *The Cathedral Within.* New York: Random House, 1999.

Watson, Robert A., and Ben Brown. *"The Most Effective Organization in the U.S.": Leadership Secrets of the Salvation Army.* New York: Crown Business, 2001.

Wood, John. *Leaving Microsoft to Change the World: An Entrepreneur's Odyssey to Educate the World's Children.* New York: Collins, 2006.

Web Resources

Alexander Technique, http://www.alexandertechnique.com

Ashoka, http://www.ashoka.org

Kristine and Richard Carlson, *Don't Sweat the Small Stuff,* http://dontsweat.com

Columbia University, The Social Enterprise Program (SEP) at Columbia Business School, http://www4.gsb.columbia.edu/socialenterprise

Craigslist, http://www.craigslist.org

Drucker Archives, http://www.druckerinstitute.com/ DruckerArchives.aspx

The Drucker Institute, http://www.druckerinstitute.com

Duke University, Center for the Advancement of Social Entrepreneurship (CASE), Duke University's Fuqua School of Business, http://www.caseatduke.org/ index.html

Bill and Melinda Gates Foundation, http://www.gates foundation.org

Greenleaf Center for Servant Leadership, http://www .greenleaf.org

Habitat for Humanity, http://www.habitat.org

Leader to Leader Institute, http://www.leadertoleader .org

Lubuto Library Project, http://www.lubuto.org

The Points of Light Institute, http://www.pointsoflight .org

Room to Read, http://www.roomtoread.org

Harriet Rubin, "Peter's Principles," *Inc.* (March 1998). Available at: http://www.inc.com/magazine/19980 301/887.html

Skoll Foundation, http://www.skollfoundation.org

Social Edge, a program of the Skoll Foundation, http:// www.socialedge.org

Special Libraries Association, http://www.sla.org

United Way, http://www.liveunited.org

VolunteerMatch, http://www.volunteermatch.org

NOTES

1. Peter F. Drucker, interview by Bruce Rosenstein, April 11, 2005, Claremont, Calif.
2. Peter F. Drucker with Joseph A. Maciariello, *Management: Revised Edition* (New York: Collins, 2008), 188.
3. Drucker, interview, April 11, 2005.
4. Peter F. Drucker, *The Age of Discontinuity: Guidelines to Our Changing Society* (1969; repr., New Brunswick, N.J.: Transaction Publishers, 1992), 264.
5. Peter F. Drucker, quoted in Elizabeth Hall, "Career Moves for Ages 20 to 70: Peter Drucker on Jobs, Life Paths, Maturity...and Freud," *Psychology Today* (November–December 1992): 54–57, 74–79 (originally published October 1968).
6. "The Icon Speaks: An Interview with Peter Drucker," *Information Outlook* (February 2002): 6–11.
7. Drucker, interview, April 11, 2005.
8. Drucker with Maciariello, *Management: Revised Edition*, 43.
9. Peter F. Drucker, *Classic Drucker: Essential Wisdom of Peter Drucker from the Pages of "Harvard Business Review"* (Boston: Harvard Business School Press, 2006), 18.
10. Peter F. Drucker, *Management Challenges for the 21st Century* (New York: HarperBusiness, 1999), 164.

11. Peter F. Drucker, interview by Bruce Rosenstein, January 7, 2003, Claremont, Calif.

12. Peter F. Drucker, *People and Performance: The Best of Peter Drucker on Management* (New York: Harper's College Press, 1977), 238.

13. Peter F. Drucker, *Managing the Non-Profit Organization: Practices and Principles* (New York: HarperBusiness, 1990), 207.

14. Drucker, "How to Be an Employee," in *People and Performance*, 269.

15. Ibid.

16. Ibid., 270.

17. Peter F. Drucker, *The Effective Executive* (1967; revised ed., New York: Collins, 2006), 101.

18. Suzanne Muchnic, "Landscapes of the Mind," *Pomona College Magazine* (Fall 1994).

19. "According to Peter Drucker," *Forbes ASAP*, March 29, 1993, 90–95.

20. Drucker with Maciariello, *Management: Revised Edition*, 345.

21. Gary Hamel and C. K. Prahalad, *Competing for the Future* (Boston: Harvard Business School Press, 1994), xxi.

22. Claremont Graduate School, "Peter F. Drucker Describes the Lessons of a Lifetime," news release, October 21, 1987.

23. Peter F. Drucker, *Drucker on Asia: A Dialogue Between Peter Drucker and Isao Nakauchi* (Oxford, Eng., and Newton, Mass.: Butterworth-Heinemann, 1997), 104.

24. Drucker, interview, April 11, 2005.

25. Drucker with Maciariello, *Management: Revised Edition*, 155.

26. Drucker, *People and Performance*, 238.

27. Peter F. Drucker, "Subject: You on Me," *NewManagement* 2, no. 3 (Winter 1985): 28–29.

28. Drucker with Maciariello, *Management: Revised Edition*, 188.

29. Drucker, interview, April 11, 2005.

30. Ibid.

31. "The Icon Speaks," 11.

32. Drucker, *The Effective Executive*, 109.

33. Peter F. Drucker, interview by Bruce Rosenstein, April 12, 2005, Claremont, Calif.

34. Bruce Rosenstein, "Scandals Nothing New to Business Guru," *USA Today*, July 5, 2002.

35. Drucker, *The Effective Executive*, 111.

36. Bruce Rosenstein, "Drucker's Reinventing Himself at Age 95," *USA Today*, November 15, 2004.

37. Drucker, interview, April 11, 2005.
38. Ibid.
39. Drucker, *Managing the Non-Profit Organization*, 201.
40. Harriet Rubin, "Peter's Principles," *Inc.* (March 1998): 62–64+, esp. 68.
41. Drucker, interview, April 11, 2005.
42. Ibid.
43. Drucker, *People and Performance*, 270.
44. Drucker, interview, April 11, 2005.
45. Ibid.
46. Drucker, interview, April 12, 2005.
47. Drucker, *Management Challenges for the 21st Century*, 74.
48. Drucker with Maciariello, *Management: Revised Edition*, 113.
49. Drucker, *Management Challenges for the 21st Century*, 188.
50. Drucker with Maciariello, *Management: Revised Edition*, 252.
51. Drucker, *Management Challenges for the 21st Century*, 189.
52. Rubin, "Peter's Principles," 64.
53. Hall, "Career Moves for Ages 20 to 70," 76.
54. Drucker, *Management Challenges for the 21st Century*, 190.
55. T. George Harris, "The Post-Capitalist Executive: An Interview with Peter F. Drucker," *Harvard Business Review* (May–June 1993): 114–22.
56. Drucker with Maciariello, *Management: Revised Edition*, 52.
57. Drucker, *Drucker on Asia*, 100–101.
58. Ibid., 101.
59. Drucker, *Managing the Non-Profit Organization*, 49.
60. Drucker, *Classic Drucker*, 176.
61. Drucker with Maciariello, *Management: Revised Edition*, 150.
62. Drucker, *Management Challenges for the 21st Century*, 191.
63. Drucker with Maciariello, *Management: Revised Edition*, 288.
64. Bruce Rosenstein, "Leading for the Future: An Interview with Richard F. Schubert," *Shine a Light/Leader to Leader* (April 2005): 23.
65. Drucker with Maciariello, *Management: Revised Edition*, 256.
66. Drucker, *Managing the Non-Profit Organization*, 42.
67. Peter F. Drucker, *Managing for the Future: The 1990s and Beyond* (New York: Truman Talley Books/Plume, 1993), 108.
68. Drucker with Maciariello, *Management: Revised Edition*, 56.
69. Peter M. Senge, *The Fifth Discipline: The Art and Practice of the Learning Organization* (New York: Currency Doubleday, 1990), 3.
70. Drucker with Maciariello, *Management: Revised Edition*, 197.

71. Rubin, "Peter's Principles," 65.
72. Peter F. Drucker, *Post-Capitalist Society* (New York: HarperBusiness, 1993), 210.
73. Drucker, interview, April 11, 2005.
74. Drucker, *Managing for the Future*, 329.

ACKNOWLEDGMENTS

There is not enough space to properly thank all the people who made this book possible, and who have enriched my life during the researching and writing of it. Some people are no longer with us, especially Peter Drucker himself, who had the patience and good humor to sit for several interviews for the book.

Any list would have to start with my wife, Deborah Goodman, for her love and support during the ups and downs of this long process, one that took longer and went through more twists and turns than either of us envisioned. I was also able to continually call on her talents as a professional editor to help me make this a better book.

Not only am I married to an editor, but my brother Jay is in the same profession. He too provided sound feedback after reading the first draft of the book.

My parents, Paul and Harriet Rosenstein, have been wonderful role models in life. They too have been very supportive of this book.

Thanks to my former editors at *USA Today*, Jacqueline Blais and Gary Rawlins, who guided and encouraged my journalistic efforts.

I cannot thank my editor, Johanna Vondeling of Berrett-Koehler, enough for all she has done. She had the vision and patience to realize there was a strong central idea in my book, but that it was not the one I originally brought to her. She also helped give the book the structure it required. The managing editor of Berrett-Koehler, Jeevan Sivasubramaniam, has displayed wonderful emotional intelligence when I have needed it the most. Thanks to everyone else at Berrett-Koehler for their hard work and care on my behalf, much of which will continue for many months to come.

Special thanks to Nancy Evans of Wilsted & Taylor Publishing Services, whose astute editorial judgment improved the book considerably.

My agent, John Willig, has been a marvel of persistence and a ready source of publishing wisdom. Along with Johanna, he is the other indispensable factor in transforming this book into a reality, and I can't thank him enough.

Thanks are also due to Tom Koulopoulos, who is not only an insightful commentator on Peter Drucker's work, but a longtime supporter of mine who introduced me to John Willig. Tom is also a perfect example of someone who lives in more than one world.

Frances Hesselbein, who wrote the foreword, put me in touch with some of the most important people I've encountered in my research. Her name magically opened doors for me to people whom I might never have met otherwise.

Many thanks to Doris Drucker for her reading of this

book in draft form. Her comments were extremely help-ful. Thanks are also due to other members of the Drucker family: Cecily Drucker, Joan Winstein, Kathleen Spivack, and Nova Spivack.

At the Drucker-Ito School and the Drucker Institute, thanks go to Ira Jackson, Bob Buford, Rick Wartzman, Zach First, Jacob High, Joseph Maciariello, Cornelis (Kees) de Kluyver, Melinda Moers Harriman, Christina Wassenaar, and many others. Many thanks to Marilyn Thomsen, whom I met while she was in public relations at the Claremont Graduate University. I first talked to her while doing a feature story on Peter Drucker for *USA Today* in 2002. She became a friend during and after her days at the school, and a trusted adviser who read the first draft of this book.

I am grateful to Duane Webster for sparking my inter-est in Drucker in 1986, in the management course Duane taught at the Catholic University of America's School of Library and Information Science.

Alan Inouye read multiple versions of my manuscripts, and provided excellent advice, helping me to think more deeply about what I really wanted to write. Many thanks are also due to more of my first readers: T. George Har-ris (and his in-depth personal knowledge as a friend and collaborator of Peter Drucker's), Lynne Perri, and Young Chul Kang. Thanks also to Berrett-Koehler's team of first readers: Jeffrey Kulick, Marcia Daszko, and especially Danielle Scott, whose comments and suggestions have greatly strengthened the final version of the book.

Finally, thanks to the many colleagues, friends, former students, and followers of Peter Drucker who shared their thoughts and experiences with me and expanded my un-derstanding of living in more than one world.

Bruce Rosenstein is a journalist and research librarian. He was with *USA Today*, in McLean, Virginia, for twenty-one years, until the final stages of writing *Living in More Than One World*. He was the "embedded Librarian" in the News section, and regularly wrote about business and management books for the newspaper's Money section.

He wrote about and interviewed Peter Drucker extensively for *USA Today*, and wrote a series of columns about him in 2001–2002 for *Information Outlook*, the publication of the Special Libraries Association/SLA. He has studied Drucker's work for more than twenty years.

In addition to *USA Today* and *Information Outlook*, Bruce has written for such publications as *Leader to Leader*, *ON-LINE*, *Library Journal*, *News Library News*, and *ARSC Journal*, a music publication. He scripted and selected the recordings for a weekly rock music radio program heard worldwide on The Voice of America, from 1974 to 1988.

He is also a lecturer in the Catholic University of America's School of Library and Information Science, in Washington, D.C.

Bruce has a BA in Communications from the American University in Washington, D.C., and an MSLS from the Catholic University of America's School of Library and Information Science.

To learn more about Bruce and *Living in More Than One World*, please visit www.brucerosenstein.com.

Visit Our Website

Go to www.bkconnection.com to read exclusive previews and excerpts of new books, find detailed information on all Berrett-Koehler titles and authors, browse subject-area libraries of books, and get special discounts.

Subscribe to Our Free E-Newsletter

Be the first to hear about new publications, special discount offers, exclusive articles, news about bestsellers, and more! Get on the list for our free e-newsletter by going to www.bkconnection.com.

Get Quantity Discounts

Berrett-Koehler books are available at quantity discounts for orders of ten or more copies. Please call us toll-free at (800) 929-2929 or email us at bkp.orders@aidcvt.com.

Host a Reading Group

For tips on how to form and carry on a book reading group in your workplace or community, see our website at www.bkconnection.com.

Join the BK Community

Thousands of readers of our books have become part of the "BK Community" by participating in events featuring our authors, reviewing draft manuscripts of forthcoming books, spreading the word about their favorite books, and supporting our publishing program in other ways. If you would like to join the BK Community, please contact us at bkcommunity@bkpub.com.

31901047152428